Autobiography of an Entrepreneur

AUTOBIOGRAPHY
of an
ENTREPRENEUR

Reflections on 20 Years of Travel, Adventure & Starting Businesses

JESSE KRIEGER

Write to
Jesse@JesseKrieger.com to connect with the author.

Notice: Some names have been changed to respect the privacy of those involved in the stories within this book.

ISBN:

Contents

Introduction

In writing this book I have taken the advice that I've given countless authors over the years: *Write the Introduction last*. So here I am on the tail end of a manic 10-week writing sprint in which I've cranked out over 64,000 words chronicling the last 20 years of travels, adventures, and starting businesses. For me the writing process is just about at an end, and for you the journey is about begin. If you picked up this book because something about the word entrepreneur electrifies and excites you, you're in the right place. If you picked up this book to get insight into what it's like to spend two decades traveling the world, chasing ideas wherever they lead, and starting businesses when an idea is too compelling not to, then you are definitely in the right place. And if you picked up this book because somewhere on our journeys of life our stories crossed and you're curious what it's been like to live my life in the driver seat, then hop in—you're riding shotgun, friend! This book is the answer to all the times I've been asked what my next book will be, and all the times I wondered if I was destined to be a one-book author, despite publishing over 100 books by others. It has been surprisingly fun to recount the wild ride that is my life, and I hope you're pleasantly surprised while reading it.

Autobiography of an Entrepreneur is a tip of the literary hat to Paramahansa Yogananda, who wrote *Autobiography of a Yogi.* He lived a life of magic and miracles, spanning the globe and positively impacting countless people. This book is a first-hand account of the formative stories in his life, where you can peer inside his mind and understand how he saw the world, in order to understand the man behind the worldly accomplishments. Likewise, I have approached this book as a window into my soul, sharing the key movements in the symphony of my life so that you may see, hear, and feel the way I lived it. In this spirit, I hope you are moved by the majesty of each moment and that you are inspired to set the stage for your own coronation. This is not a how-to book, and there is no secret formula to be revealed. But for the keen reader and the eager entrepreneur, there is a lifetime of wisdom within these pages, and I'll consider it a success if you choose to take action on a dream as a result of reading.

For the last 20 years, I have made it my life's work to follow my interests and passions wherever they lead and to put a business model behind them when the opportunities arose. Accordingly, I have been an entrepreneur my entire adult life. Never once have I been an employee; never once have I had a "job." Well, I should say never in my *adult* life. There was one time when I was 16 that I roasted nuts and scooped ice cream at the mall for a couple months to save up for a stereo. My dad would take off work to come watch me, amazed to witness me actually "work." But since I turned 18 and moved away from the town I grew up in, it's been a barrage of business ideas made manifest, a passport stamped full from travels, then another, and another. Has it always been easy? Absolutely not! Have I been beneficiary to some amazingly encouraging parents, mentors, investors, partners, friends, and business owners? You bet. From as far back as I can remember, I had resolved to live life on my own terms. And when that wasn't possible or dangling just out of reach, I dug deep, hustled hard, tried a million things, and found a few that worked.

When I was growing up, I loved to read *Choose Your Own Adventure* books, where you'd read a scene and then choose what you wanted to do next. The result of that choice set the story in motion in a vastly different way than it would have otherwise run if another option was taken. That is how my story goes, choosing in to one adventure after another. With each one, the story twists and turns, evolves and expands, and leads to a new set of choices that weren't even on the table before. Then, when the spirit so moved me, I would choose a new adventure and bid farewell to the past as responsibly and ethically as possible. Being willing to let go of what had become familiar is the other side of choosing a new adventure and life feeling brand new. In such a fashion I truly feel that I have lived a number of lives, each self-contained in the context, creations, actions, and accomplishments that defined each era.

To put that another way, from age 14 to 24, everyone in my life knew my dream to be a rock guitarist. I carried my Fender Stratocaster everywhere, learning Jimi Hendrix lick for lick and making my first recordings on a 4-track cassette player in my childhood bedroom. Following the music took me from Los Angeles to London, from Vienna, Austria to Nashville, Tennessee, and then across America in a tour van, twice. From there I chose a new adventure and entered the world of business, becoming a consultant, then an investment banker, then taking a company public in my twenties without a degree. The creativity I loved in music transposed to turning ideas into reality in business, and I founded or co-founded five companies in my twenties. A life-long love of learning landed me at the top public university in the world, and I excelled in academics and Chinese language, earning a number of degrees. A curiosity to understand women and become an attractive man led to an international career as a dating coach, ultimately being flown around the world to teach seminars and take groups of guys to nightclubs to meet women. My love of books came to the fore when I put pen to paper the first time and wrote my first. Then I fell in love with supporting authors and published over 100 books by other authors and entrepreneurs.

The common thread that ties these diverse and decorous experiences together is the belief that anything is possible with enough work and ingenuity. My life has been a living laboratory to test that hypothesis every which way. Sometimes with dramatic effect and the ecstasy of accomplishing a dream; others with the equally dramatic effect of flat-out failures that knocked me down for the count. But I have always ascribed to Winston Churchill's definition that success is moving from one failure to the next with no loss of enthusiasm. Win or lose, I keep spinning the wheel of life and seeing where it takes me next. As you turn the page, you'll embark on my account of where it's taken me thus far. Enjoy!

Let's Start from the Top

The original title for this book was "Who Am I...Really?", which I believe to be the most interesting question one can ask themselves. "Who am I...really?" is so rich, so loaded with possibility and potential, and potentially the most vexing question ever. Go ahead. Give it a try. If you're going to read this book, you get to play along; ask yourself here and now, "Who am I...really?" and see what comes up for you. Assuming you did it, and paused for more than a breath to actually consider the implications, it's quite fascinating what comes back, isn't it?

For the last ten years since I wrote my first book, *Lifestyle Entrepreneur*, and went on to build an eponymous publishing house, supporting over 100 authors achieve their dream of becoming published, I have often wondered whether I would put the proverbial paper to pad once more to write another book. Throughout that journey I've had an insider's view into what this magical process really entails and how every author must face this same question in their own way as they write and as their words become imminently part of the permanent record. Oh yes, publishing a book is much like opening Pandora's Box; you can try to close the lid again, but there is no way to put all that escaped in the precious time it was open back in the cage. As such, both myself and every other author get the pleasure (or excruciating agony) or sitting with this existential question: "Who am I…really?"

To ask "Who am I?" is pretty straightforward, at least at the surface level. It's easy to associate identity with the current iteration of our life's expression. I'm an author, I'm a publisher, I'm a man, I'm a homeowner, I'm a son, a brother, an uncle. But when you add in that "…really?", it begins to probe a little bit deeper below those surface-level expressions. Put another way, each identity I stated in the previous sentence is true, but none are all-encompassing or complete. That is why the twist is to allow yourself to peek below those visible and obvious manifestations to witness the vast wilderness that lives beyond. Consider as well that each of these identities that we wear, such as "I'm an author," is true now but may not have been previously. I wasn't before I wrote my first book. So, am I an author…really? Is that the epitome of my beingness with which I uniquely and totally identify? Of course not, even if it is useful as a simple answer when the moment holds the question simply.

In this book we are going to follow this thread of "…really?" all the way down the rabbit hole. As far as there is a light prompting us forward and illuminating further revelation, we will go. But what gets even more interesting is when we continue forward with conscious awareness after all the formalities and familiarities fade from view. When we have ventured beyond the realms of the ordinary, the interesting, indeed even the enthralling answers, we continue on. By definition, that which is beyond the known is the unknown, and so I'll be honest up front that as I write these opening words, I don't yet know where we will wind up on the other side. What I can promise is that the stories and strategies in this book will expand your perspective of what's possible and—as it is my great hope—inspire you to answer this question in new, unexpected, and absolutely profound ways: "Who am I...really?" If it doesn't, you have my blessing to return the book and leave me a bad review.

So, let's get into it. I'll go first and use the prismatic events of my life as a starting prompt. In so doing, let's set aside any pretense, cut short the preamble, and get right into the good stuff, shall we?

Who am I...really? is the thought that entered my mind, contorted on the floor of a yoga studio on the west side of Las Vegas one fateful Summer night in 2022. Devastated by the loss of a business I spent nearly a decade building, my mind was wandering while my body was bent like a pretzel. It's not the first time I've entertained the question, far from it, but this time it came in response to another question I had been pondering for some time: "If I were to write another book, what would it be about?" My first book opens with a scene from Koh Phangan, Thailand, heading back out to the Full Moon Party at 4:00 a.m. after what had already been a fun and festive night of partying on the beach. Bass thumping, neon lights, revelers from around the world gathered to celebrate life under the full moon illuminating the beach like an unblinking spectral cyclops.

When I asked the question then—*10 years ago*—the answers were fun to recite. I was a recent bestselling author in the country of Malaysia, in the midst of a book tour across Southeast Asia speaking at book fairs, or as I liked to say, "shaking hands, signing books, and kissing babies". In a tribute to the literary essence that comprises *Lifestyle Entrepreneur* I planned a four-day interlude with some of my best friends in Thailand before continuing the second leg of the book tour, which wrapped up on top of a mountain overlooking the lush tropical terraces of Penang. Sitting there with my amazing editor and a few staff from Kanyin Publications, I raised a toast, took a sip, and marveled at how I got to answer the question "Who am I...really?" on that fine day.

That was 2012, and now it's 2022. Then I was 30; now I'm 40. Ten laps around the sun later, and I'm still alive and kicking. Still probing at life with the forceps of foresight; still analyzing each brilliant expression of the ever-unfolding present moment with tenderness and a touch of flair. It's astonishing to think of just how much has transpired between then and now, and yet even that 10-year period is only 25 percent of my life thus far, and this decade I've just entered into is the waypoint of what my genetics would determine as a halfway point of sorts across the entire span of this lifetime here on this beautiful Earth Mother, the best school and perpetual teacher we all get to share.

Back then, "Who am I...really?" would read something like this. I was a recent graduate from UC Berkeley, although I hadn't even started school until age 26. Before that I spent a decade in love with music, living in LA, Vienna, Austria, London, and Nashville, where I was lead guitarist in a rock band and co-founder of a record label—my first business at age 21! My two and half years as a full-time student stands as the only time in my adult life I haven't been in some stage of starting and running businesses. Twenty years of entrepreneurship started on Music Row in Nashville, producing artists in our homespun recording studio through all hours of the night

Growing up I was never seriously interested in business, I was all guitar, all day long. Ditching high school to learn Jimi Hendrix songs note for note was way more my jam than calculus and biology. After high school I moved to LA and attended Los Angeles

Music Academy, a one-year guitar program with no academics. It was amazing. Playing music non-stop, putting together a cover band, and playing out in LA. At ages 18 and 19, I had big black X's on my hands going into bars and clubs, and back then, we had to guarantee the bars that we'd bring out a certain number of people or we would have to pay them to play there. Not exactly the rock star dream, just yet.

One great thing at Los Angeles Music Academy was that 80 percent of the student body was international. So, all of a sudden, I found myself learning about Japan over lunch one day, Germany the next, Brazil another. Bonded by our love of music, our class of around 30 became fast friends and one year felt like a lifetime in and of itself.

Looking back, I credit those international friendships with cracking open an interest to travel, and so as the year wound down in LA, I decided to join five of my high school friends on a two-month trip to Europe. Although I was constantly in bands in LA and was becoming a better guitarist every day, it wasn't exactly lucrative to be paying clubs on Sunset to perform, and I was still years away from even being able to order a beer in those same bars and clubs. It was an easy choice to accept a belated graduation present from my dad to pay for flights and a Eurail pass to go live in hostels with my childhood friends.

Our flight out was scheduled on September 14, 2001, and in the final days of our pre-departure preparations, the whole world changed on September 11 as airplanes slammed into the World Trade Center in New York and the Pentagon, with another headed for perhaps the White House. A mixture of absolute shock and horror at what was unfolding threw into question whether or not our flight would even take off. As it turns out, our flight was one of the first to depart after nearly all commercial aircraft were grounded in the chaotic aftermath of that tragic day.

So, at 19 years old, fresh in the aftermath of September 11, we were off to Europe for two months. It turned out to be a real eye-opener to witness the aftermath and America's march to war from overseas. I remember sitting in a bar in Paris watching President Bush announce the invasion of Afghanistan and wondering aloud at what was going on in the world and what it meant to be American. There were occasional protests and demonstrations in the streets across the European capitals we visited, but being 19 years old and in Europe with friends, we didn't get wrapped up in the patriotic and militaristic fervor that was unfolding in the USA. We simply experienced each day as a new adventure, in a new country, with new friends, making memories and generally having the time of our lives

In the course of that trip, I met an American guy from Florida who had been playing guitar on the streets for nearly seven months, making his living like a modern-day troubadour. We instantly hit it off. Naturally, I had brought a backpacking guitar with me to Europe—a tiny instrument with no headstock but that was still technically a real guitar. We jammed in the park together for our friends in Vienna, Austria...then got a gig playing at a bar for free food, free drinks, and a couple hundred schillings. We had a blast, but then were off to the next destination on our travels.

On the last day of our trip before we were scheduled to travel back to Paris from Nice, France, my friends and I were doing our thing, drinking and partying reflecting on the amazing memories made in just eight short weeks. As the bar closed and we were hustled out onto the cobblestone streets of Southern France, a big group of around 10 guys came up and started getting really aggressive. One thing led to another, and we basically got our asses kicked in a back alley of Nice. In a daze, with fists flying and the situation escalating out of control, someone smashed a wine bottle on my head, sending a huge splattering of blood down my face and all over my shirt. Eventually, we got away from them and were making our way back to our hostel, looking over our shoulders and making sure they didn't come back, or that police didn't stumble across us in our sorry state. I remember thinking to myself, *This can't be how our epic summer trip ends...*

In that moment of peril, bruised and battered with a blood-stained shirt and my friends in a similar state, I made a decision that set the course of my life on a path that ultimately leads to this book. I decided to skip my ticket back to America and take my chances living in Europe. I figured I could go back to Vienna and reconnect with the musician friend I met there and figure something out. All I knew was that the idea of going home beaten up to move back in with my parents sounded like a defeat I wasn't willing to wager. I told my friends, and characteristically, they didn't believe me for a second. Hard to blame them, but it became real when we arrived at the train platform and they all loaded up to head to Paris for the return flight. I stood right there on that platform and waved goodbye as their faces turned from disbelief, to wondering "What the hell?", to the whistle blowing, the doors closing, and then *whoosh*—the train was gone, and I was standing on that platform all alone, with a throbbing head, thinking, *OK, wow, this is about to get real interesting.*

And interesting it was! "Who am I...really?" got answered that day as the 19-year-old Jesse skipped his flight home to take his chances in Europe. 2001 was long before the age of iPhones, and the extent of my technological capabilities was having a Hotmail account to write emails to my family about my travels abroad. In other words, the world wasn't yet at our fingertips, and it took a little bit of sleuthing to figure out how to take trains all the way back to Vienna from South of France, but I figured it out, arrived at the youth hostel where my musician friend Scott was living, and collapsed in a heap on the floor somewhere around 5:00 a.m. a day or two later.

I could probably write a whole book on what happened that year, and honestly it would be a pretty epic book in and of itself. Living in a student dorm hostel in Vienna, two blocks from Westbahnhof train station, Scott and I quickly became a dynamic duo, playing music on the streets and eventually in bars and clubs around Vienna. I remember when I moved there, Austria was still using schillings, and after New Year's 2002, the euro came into existence. This was a big deal, as the euro had coins for worth one and two euros each, and people not being familiar with the price difference perhaps didn't value those as much as the schilling coins we used to get for tips before. In any event, we were living well, with rent of 170 euros that we earned from one show or a few afternoons playing on the streets. We each had a drawer filled with coins and would just grab a handful of money and go out to explore the town. Every week or two, I'd walk two blocks, hop on a train, and go visit a new country. It was magic, pure and simple.

My dad thought it was the coolest thing ever that I decided to stay in Europe. My mom was understandably worried but ultimately supportive and enjoyed getting my lengthy emails describing the daily sights and sounds of Europe for the better part of a year. Month after month, it was music, travel, and learning little bits about languages and cultures that were all brand new. Put another way, one year prior, I couldn't have pointed to Austria on a map, but now it was my home base, and the rest of Europe was a train ride away. We turned the basement of the student dorm into a recording studio, and my dad sent out my Fender Stratocaster and a digital 8-track recorder to play with. Scott and I would recruit musicians from Vienna's world-class classical music universities, and we'd record songs with violins, cellos, oboes, saxophones, you name it. We made our own CDs and sold them at impromptu hostel parties, where we would, of course, perform as well, selling beers for one euro each that we bought for a quarter. Life was just a musical party in myriad shapes and forms.

At one point we got invited to moonlight at SAE Vienna, the School of Audio Engineering. Our friend Niko, a wild, hilarious Austrian dude with dreadlocks who loved death metal was studying there and said we could come record from midnight to 6:00 a.m. for free. Since we didn't have anything resembling a normal schedule anyhow, the timing was perfect and we went back and forth to the professional recording studio in the still of the Viennese night. This was the first time I got a real taste of recording in a professional studio for more than just a couple hours at a time. I became fascinated by the production side of music and came to appreciate how audio engineering and mixing was an art in and of itself. Getting a basic grasp of music production only fueled my creativity, and we recorded dozens of songs between our makeshift basement studio at the student dorm and the professional SAE studio.

For the better part of a year I was a street musician, living in a student dorm without a visa, traveling across borders frequently enough where that didn't matter, and not working in any type of job that required papers; I existed in this nether realm of legality without actually needing papers to live in Vienna and Europe for a year after skipping my ticket home.

When I finally felt the call to make a next move, I figured, "Why not apply to School of Audio Engineering in Nashville and take a deep dive into the production side of making music?" I had placed in a songwriting contest hosted by a record label in Nashville and always knew that it was "Music City," which was about all the argument I needed to pick up shop and move there.

Heading to Nashville, TN - Music City, USA

Once I made the decision to decamp from Europe and step into the next stage of life, a countdown timer began and the energy shifted from carefree days biking along the Danube and sampling Turkish delights in Vienna's abundant open-air markets to thinking of what else I wanted to do before flying back to the States. It was the summer of 2002, and the student dorm we were living in had converted to a youth hostel. I remember fondly sitting in the lobby, playing guitar, and hanging out with the Hungarian crew that ran the hostel—just laughing and having fun. We decided to throw a going away party. Actually, it was more of a series of going away parties leading up to the day I actually walked those fateful two blocks to Westbahnhof and got on a train, this time not to return just a few hours or days later. But given the fact that I skipped my ticket home now close to a year ago, a fact well-known among my friends, there was a running joke and maybe a few side bets as to whether I'd actually leave or not. Highly understandable.

For those last halcyon weeks of summer we wove an ever-evolving tapestry of music, laughter, magic, and memories. Scott and

I would buy a shopping cart full of beer at the Billa supermarket and wheel it two blocks up the street to the Haus Burgenland II (the official name of the hostel), put them in the fridge, and then break them out each evening with a revolving door of street musicians, world travelers, a handful of locals, and the occasional circus performer. One standout memory involves a guy named Cyrus, who was traveling with a circus, holding an eight-inch nail up to his nose, then having guests from the party come and bang it up his nose with the butt of an axe. To this day, I don't know how he didn't puncture his brain and collapse, but it made for one hell of a party trick! Another memory was having learned "The Rain Song" by Led Zeppelin note-for-note, spending days in the basement studio drilling it time and again, just to have a visiting Icelandic guy celebrating a birthday make an impassioned request that what he wanted more than anything else was to hear "The Rain Song." Pleasantly surprised with the request, which is hardly the type of song someone yells out to hear at a nightclub, I said I'd be happy to oblige and proceeded to hold the room in rapt attention as I finessed the strings like Jimmy Page and pulled out each note like a drop of rain from musical heaven. It gives me goosebumps as I write this to think of playing that big final chord and hearing the whole room erupt into applause and cheers.

Such were the final days of my time in Vienna and Europe. I was 20 years old and felt like I had lived and entire life in that one year. A life that would have been stillborn had I got on the train from Nice with my friends and returned home bruised, battered, and licking my wounds. Now it was a revolving door of musical mayhem until my final departure, and this time I did keep my flight and made it back to the States without incident. I visited my family in the San Francisco Bay Area and caught up with my friends for a few days, regaling them with stories and pouring through piles of pictures before taking possession of my sister's Jeep Cherokee for the drive across America to Music City, USA.

With my guitar in tow, a suitcase full of clothes, and not much else I set off on a road trip to Nashville, stopping at epic desert vistas to watch the sunset and write songs. Sleeping in cheap hotels and both enjoying the journey while also making decent time to arrive for orientation. Then, before I knew it, the next chapter of life had arrived full force. Walking into School of Audio Engineering Nashville on Music Circle, just a stone's throw from half of the major record labels and music publishing houses in the country, was a far cry from moonlighting at SAE Vienna just a few months prior. It was *way* cooler!

I dove into learning music production with a passion. In fact, my class was the final class that learned how to edit two-inch tape, as we were at the dawn of the Pro Tools era and digital music production was becoming more widespread in 2002. Looking back, it's wild to think that the Jimi Hendrix records I grew up listening to were edited by physically cutting two-inch magnetic tape and "taping" it back together—quite an art and a science to make sure you get the edit done on the right beat! Not to be too nostalgic, since digital music production was leaps and bounds easier than scrubbing the reels of tape machines with a wax pencil and razor blade as your tools of the trade. There were definitely two camps at that time, the analog purists and the forward-looking producers that were embracing digital developments as soon as they came online.

For me, it was all great learning, and I'm glad to have at least had a season of learning analog before diving headlong into digital production, eventually working up to being able to make edits on Pro Tools as fast as my fingers could fly across the keyboard.

The first few months in Nashville were a blur; sleeping on the couch at a student's house until I could find a more long-term place to live and studying and making music every day. It was there at SAE that I met Jake Harsh, my band mate and first business partner, and we went on to move in together on Music Row, turn the middle floor of the house we rented into a studio, and record all the time. We'd have local gospel musicians and R&B guys that were making the rounds performing in Nashville over and cut tracks in our living room and kitchen until the sun came up. Music Row is actually two streets of beautiful Old World Southern houses that barely anyone lived in; they were all converted into music publishing houses and record labels. I actually think the term music publishing "house" was born on Music Row, as these businesses were run out of houses. Going into 2003, we lived right next door to one that had a deal with Kings of Leon, and they were just making waves with their first record. I'd go to Starbucks and run into Keith Urban; drive down the street and see Allison Kraus coming out of a recording session; rehearse at SIR and pass Dolly Parton in the hallway. It was the funnest little town feel in the few square blocks where so much music came out of, on the other side of the railroad tracks from downtown and the city center.

In the midst of writing, recording, producing, playing open mics, and oh yeah, attending classes at SAE, we started to make a little name for ourselves in the midst of Music City. Jake and I started as a songwriting duo; he played rhythm and sang, and I played lead guitar and helped come up with melodies and experimental sounds. I got a baritone guitar, which has a longer neck and thicker strings, and started playing it with a cello bow with a delay pedal that would swell the sounds and shriek like a banshee. I had an e-bow electromagnet that continuously vibrated the strings and made sounds that you just couldn't get from playing with a pick or fingers. Thus were the origins of Harsh Krieger, and soon enough we recruited a dedicated bass and drum player and were a full-blown rock band. We thought the name sounded cool, something like Led Zeppelin where at first it doesn't make sense, then it eventually just rolls off the tongue. Also it roughly meant "fierce warrior" in German, a nice little throwback to my time in Europe.

The School of Audio Engineering was just a nine-month program, and it seemed to fly by. A great experience and just the right catalyst to kick my musical inclinations into high gear, on both sides of the glass; performing and producing. Once SAE was over, our schedules quickly filled out to 12 to 14 hours of music just about every day. Harsh Krieger was our main focus, but it was still a revolving door of musicians, producing tracks for other artists, having producers bring over new gear we could try out, and sometimes just jamming for the fun of it all night long. As a band we started to focus on playing out more and working our way up to getting headlining gigs at the top spots like Mercy Lounger and Exit/In. We got a booking agent, had a musician friend run sound for us at the clubs so we sounded good, and took each opportunity to grow and evolve as musicians and bandmates.

Now it was 2003, and I was finally 21. After living in Europe where there were practically no age limits on buying alcohol, I could finally go to a bar in the USA and order a drink—and I didn't need a big black "X" on the back of my hand to go inside and perform. It was around this time that the idea of starting our own record label really grew on me. From talking with other musicians and meeting a few bands that were signed to labels, it was unclear how much support we'd really get from a label. As I started researching the business side of music, I uncovered no shortage of horror stories—artists losing the rights to their music, getting signed to a deal just to be dropped before they even released an album, and much more. This is not to say there aren't quality record labels out there, and to this day some of my heroes are record men like Clive Davis or Arista and Barry Gordy of Motown, but the more I looked into it, the more I became convinced that we should take matters into our own hands and at least have some semblance of control over our musical career.

Convincing Jake, on the other hand, was a little trickier than convincing myself. Not that he was outright opposed to the idea, but he is one of the most creative people I've ever met and lives in the world of songwriting, performing, singing, playing, and producing. Those were his passions, and it was the perfect skill set for a lead singer. I had grown up getting exposure to business, even if it wasn't my personal passion at the time. My dad runs a CPA firm and had built a list of clients who loved him personally and deeply valued his tax advice, so I got the benefit of learning about all different kinds of businesses over family dinners and conversations over the years. Learning about businesses through the lens of which ones made money and which ones lost money, from a tax perspective, certainly had some influence on my burgeoning interest in starting a label of our own versus "signing a deal" and becoming a glorified employee for another.

I started researching how to write a business plan. I went back to SAE and asked for introductions to anyone working at record labels that I could learn from and I asked my dad to make a few introductions to his consultant clients who had a good general understanding about the inner workings of a successful business. Then I brought it all to Jake and built a case for why we'd be better off running our own label, even if Harsh Krieger was the only band on the label, and he eventually agreed when I said I'd be responsible for all the business operations so he could focus on the creative side of our band and the visual branding for everything we did together. So it was at age 21 I filed the papers for Tabula Rasa Records, Inc. in Nashville, Tennessee, with a business address on Music Row and my life as a creative entrepreneur began in earnest.

Harsh Krieger Signs to Tabula Rasa Records

After forming the record label infrastructure, we promptly signed ourselves as the first and only band on the label. There was no big glamorous signing party with champagne popping off, but now we could enter agreements with people as a real business instead of just another group of guys trying to make it in Music City. I assembled a brain trust with the help of my father's introductions to his long-time client friends, forming an advisory board to help us create a real business plan and raise some money. If I thought 12 to 14 hours a day of pure music was a lot, now I was adding learning about business presentations, accounting software, and negotiating agreements to my repertoire.

One of my dad's close friends Michael Doyle heard about what we were doing and offered to fly out to Nashville for a couple days of strategic planning. Michael was the bestselling author of *Making Meetings Work* and founder of Innovation Associates, which did large-scale consulting with companies like Ford on creating new products and lines of business within their organizations. Michael sat down with Jake and I and took us through an exercise. He said, "Set your watch for three years in the future. Now get a clear picture of what you accomplished over the last three years and describe it to me in detail, using past-tense language, as though it's already happened."

Jake and I let ourselves dream big: "We celebrated out first Gold Record." "We got invited to the Grammys." "We toured the country and had songs on MTV." "We drive down the road and hear our songs on the radio..." Those were some of the grandiose visions that rolled off our tongues!

"That's great. Keep going," Michael would entreat us. "So tell me, how did it happen? What was the sequence of events that made it all real?"

While we kept talking, he was writing all over a huge piece of paper that we wrapped around our living room walls, sketching, taking notes, and telling us to keep talking until we finally exhausted our creative emanations. The result was he helped us craft a strategic plan, born from our big dreams and distilled down to weekly and monthly milestones that would let us know we were on track.

Wow, that was actually fun! I remember thinking, pleasantly surprised that business wasn't entirely boring work relative to making music. In fact, it is incredibly empowering to put detail to your dreams and to have a clear vision of the ultimate goal, while identifying what to work on today, tomorrow, and next week. Talking about it all as though it had already happened was a creative trick Michael had used with Fortune 500 companies to get them out of their heads and into their creativity, and it worked equally well for an indie record label and rock band. It can work just as well for you too, by the way. Just ask yourself, "Who am I...really?" from a point in the future looking back on the present and let yourself dream big, then fill in the details and get after it.

The strategic plan that we created became the basis for an actual business plan. That business plan became a living, breathing document that we shopped around, solicited feedback on, and eventually utilized when we asked for people to support our dream by investing in us. Over the next six months, we succeeded in raising just over $100,000, which was enough to produce our album, pay our band and road manager a meager salary, and to get a proper touring van and trailer. We made a deal with a rock music producer to create our eponymous first album, and then started splitting our time between writing and rehearsing on Music Row and heading to the old Ford Motor Factory in a sketchy part of town where the producer's studio was. The surrounding area near the old car factory was pretty rough, but once we were inside behind two sets of bolted steel doors, we were in our own world of creative magic. The brick walls, hardwood floors, and 30-inch-high ceilings were the perfect environment to record music, and the producer we were working with was living in the studio, fully immersed in the creative lifestyle like we were.

As nights turned into days, writing, recording, mixing, overdubbing and listening to versions of our songs, I couldn't help but smile at the fact that this was an echo of moonlighting at SAE Vienna just a couple short years earlier. But now, instead of walking home at sunrise to a student dorm, we would drive back to our Music Row pad and fall sleep listening to mixes of Harsh Krieger songs before hitting the road to play shows around the South on the weekends. Our blast radius expanded out from Nashville to Memphis, Atlanta, Louisville, Birmingham, Indianapolis, Cincinnati, Raleigh-Durham, and more. As our record got closer to completion, it was pretty cool to see our strategic plan and creative vision come to life. Supporting that vision was a growing team of booking agents, a band manager, our producer, and soon enough, a radio promotions team too.

Through a series of conversations, chance meetings, fastidious follow-up, and a "do whatever it takes" attitude, I eventually got us into a conversation with a subsidiary of Sony Records that worked with indie labels to distribute their albums into retailers. Back then the biggest thing going was to get into Tower Records and have music on MTV, or at least that's how I thought of it. So, I pushed hard to get the Sony subsidiary interested in telling them we were in consideration to have our music licensed for airplay on MTV, and then would pitch TV producers that made shows for MTV and tell them we were about to sign a distribution deal with Sony so they should license our music. That little game resembled the perennial question, or "Which came first, the chicken or the egg?" Would we get radio play and MTV exposure to tip the scales in our favor for a distribution deal, or would getting our record in-stores be the catalyst for more exposure on the media?

In the span of a few weeks, it all came together. We signed a deal with Bunim-Murray Productions that produced *The Real World*, *Road Rules*, and other popular shows on MTV, licensing our forthcoming record for use on any shows they produced. Meanwhile, Sony's subsidiary gave us a distribution deal so that Tabula Rasa Records would be able to release *Harsh Krieger* in stores nationwide. While that was all going on, we were in the final mixing and mastering stages for the album itself, playing shows every week and pushing our booking agents and team to arrange for a tour to support the album launch.

A Spiritual Journey in Bolivia and Peru

In the midst of all the action and excitement leading up to our record coming out, my family invited me to join them for a spiritual pilgrimage of sorts in Bolivia and Peru. Since my teenage years my dad has been on a journey of spiritual awakening. After he and my mom divorced when I was around 10 years old, he dated a number of spiritually inclined women in San Francisco and Marin County. Throughout my teens, when it was time for my sister and me to stay with our dad for a few days, that was an adventure in and of itself. We would stay over at his girlfriend's houses, often times free to roam around and explore the neighborhood into the evening with his blessing and a few dollars to spend. He learned to fly a Cessna 172, and then our weekends became aerial adventures to dude ranches and mountain airstrips across California. One time, I remember taking the wheel of the plane and keeping a straight course for 20 minutes while he took an impromptu nap. Eventually, he met his long-time partner who had changed her name to Anahaar as a result of her own spiritual awakening.

Their first date was flying over the Golden Gate Bridge at sunset. They've been together ever since.

My dad and Anahaar moved in together, and she had two sons who were a couple years older than me. Anahaar is a psychic and was working with some celebrity clients at the time, including Sean Penn's ex-wife and the lead actor from *The Sopranos*. She helped my dad walk further down his own spiritual path, and soon they were hosting solstice and equinox gatherings at the house, playing Native American instruments and giving thanks to the four directions and Great Spirit before sharing a meal with 20 or so friends. My dad began working on a book of his own, and I'd get daily downloads about the latest revelations he had in the middle of night. From the intergalactic origins of humanity to the energetic essence that underpins all life, I got quite an earful, and he would keep going until my brain was thoroughly saturated from these esoteric concepts. Notably, his book, *The Star of Light*, was always two weeks away from being done and going to "change the world." As I write this today, a couple decades later, an author and publisher myself, this is still the case. To his credit, he's just excited now as he was then.

While I was off living in Europe, then starting a rock band in Nashville, they were becoming more intrigued with visiting spiritual destinations on the planet and had dreamed up quite an adventure. They located a shaman named Mallku, who had written a book called *Machu Picchu Forever*, and hired him to lead a group of their spiritually minded friends on a sacred pilgrimage from La Paz, Bolivia to Machu Picchu, Peru. Unable to resist the call of another adventure in a faraway place, I gladly accepted their invitation to join and was whisked away to La Paz, which sits around 12,000 feet above sea level. The difference from homely, humid Music

Row to this distant capital on top of the world was dramatic, but that was just the beginning.

We journeyed to sacred sites in Bolivia, spent a night on Island of the Sun (Isla Del Sol) in the middle of Lake Titicaca, and took part in a fire-walking ceremony under the stars. My sister and I ventured off and walked 10 miles through mud hut villages to Copacabana to reunite with the group and eat traditional Bolivian dishes with fish caught just a few feet from where we sat. Making our way overland into Peru, we wound our way through the Sacred Valley of the Incas to Ollantaytambo and caught the train towards the base of Machu Picchu. Learning about the indigenous cultures and venturing off the beaten path brought back memories of riding my bike far outside Vienna into small towns and exploring along the Danube to distant tributaries, just to catch a train back at dusk, albeit on the other side of the world.

My sister and I opted to hike the Inca Trail and rendezvous with our family and travel companions inside Machu Picchu at dawn three days later. We had a guide and a sherpa for the hike, and it was the most beautiful and brutal hike I had ever done. Hiking up and down 2,500 feet of elevation changes, exploring deep into the Andes and visiting ancient archeological ruins along the way, I was in a state of bliss, in love with life and merging fully into the moment amidst the dramatic mountain scenery. Whenever I thought the hike was pushing me to my limit, a Peruvian sherpa would jog briskly past us, carrying more weight than I was and wearing cloth sandals. That certainly put things in perspective, and as it turned out, there is an Incan Marathon that navigates the trail we were hiking, which Mallku had recently run!

On the day we were to arrive in Machu Picchu, we woke up at 3:00 a.m. and hiked through the thick jungle in the dark with headlamps, arriving at the Sun Gate just before dawn for the final descent into Machu Picchu. With the pre-dawn sky painted a thousand colors and alpacas lazily roaming the hillsides, munching on grass, we trekked down into the ruins and reunited with our family just as the sun was coming up. Facing the sunrise, the first rays illuminated the faces of our travel party and we soaked in the experience for all it was worth. Then we sat in a circle on the lush grass in the midst of the ancient city and Mallku shared a Peruvian sacrament called Huachuma, a strong-tasting, thick beverage made from the San Pedro cactus with psychoactive properties.

As if the Inca Trail hike wasn't magical enough, that day lives on indelibly impressed on the recesses of my mind. Walking through magical Machu Picchu barefoot, running my hands along the stone walls, imagining what it was like to live here hundreds of years ago, with the same medicinal sacrament that has been used for generations illuminating my mind's eye. I felt a deep connection to this incredible place, and back in 2004, visitors were more or less free to roam through the ruins without supervision. The sun high overhead, the winding river wrapping around the mountain thousands of feet below, Machu Picchu is hidden in plain sight and a true wonder to behold. In a word, incredible!

The culmination of the day and the highlight of the entire trip was staying inside Machu Picchu after the park closed. As the author of *Machu Picchu Forever*, Mallku was well respected by the natives and had some special relationships in place that allowed us access to such an exclusive experience. We sat next to the Intihuatana stone—the *Hitching Post of the Sun*—under a sky full of stars, the only people in the entire ancient city, while Mallku prepared a small fire and chanted songs while flapping a condor's feather to feed the flames. Words escape me to convey the pure magic of that moment, but I can see and feel it as clearly now as I experienced it then nearly 20 years ago.

Years later, I returned to the Sacred Valley of the Incas as part of a men's group called Entrepreneurs Awakening, with a video crew sent by Fast Company. We spent a week deep in the Andes drinking Huachuma and Ayahuasca with a medicine man named Javier, who I formed a deep connection with and eventually published no fewer than five of his books on indigenous plant medicines and their profound effects...

Touring America with Harsh Krieger

Back from Bolivia and Peru, it was time to see our labor of love through to the full glory of its creative potential. Wearing jewelry from the Andes, a skin-tight leather jacket, and skinny jeans with flat-ironed hair, I must have looked like a medicine man/rock n' roller hybrid. I was happy, refreshed, and ready for action. As we put the finishing touches on our album, time in the studio went from creative mayhem and passionate confrontations between Jake and me, and us collectively against our producer, to a more tranquil affair. There is something alive, combustible, and explosive about writing and recording rock music. We embodied that fully, even though it meant losing our tempers with each other once in a while. In the home stretch, we rallied around a shared goal. This amazing album was being born, and now all the songs fit together like a puzzle. We could see the final few pieces, and it was just about getting them in the right place.

One of those final touches was adding string sections to some of our songs. We had become friends with a string duo in Nashville called The G-Strings, a lively violinist and cellist that knew how to rock. We invited them to the studio and, with barely one listen through each track, laid down what I consider breathtakingly good string sections. They would record as a duo, then overdub themselves harmonizing with the parts they had just played. The net effect was a handful of our songs now had a four-part string section accompanying the guitar, vocals, bass, and drums. We pulled the verse and chorus string arrangements off of one song, "The Shore," and added it as a stand-alone track that led into the full song, appropriately titling it "String Interlude" in the very middle of the album. That was the proverbial cherry on top, and the album was done!

We rehearsed constantly and continued playing shows in Nashville while plotting our tour across America to coincide with our album release. When the day came, we loaded up the van and trailer on Music Row and drove 40 hours non-stop to Flagstaff, Arizona, for the first show of our West Coast tour leg. This was 2005, and I was running our label operations from a Blackberry sitting shotgun in a van, peeling away the miles across America in between shows. From Flagstaff to Phoenix, to Las Vegas, to Southern California, we wound up on Sunset Strip ready to play a showcase at The Viper Room, a rock n' roll hot spot at the time, which was owned by Johnny Depp. After setting up and sound check, I took a moment and walked outside, glancing first at our name on the marquee, then across the street to Cat Club where nearly five years earlier I was getting a black "X" on the back of my hand and guaranteeing the club booker that we'd bring 20 people or pay them the difference. It was a moment of standing outside of time and space, marveling at who I was then and answering the question anew: "Who am I… really, now?"

That fine day, the answer was lead guitarist of Harsh Krieger, rocking out at a showcase our manager and booking agent set up with a bunch of music industry folks in LA. Drawing my cello bow across the strings, throwing my head back, and raising my guitar to the roof and dropping it in time with the drums. Glancing over and seeing the veins in Jake's neck popping out as he hit the high notes full force, then facing each other and dancing around in rhythm before the next verse. Then, a montage of handshakes, pictures, profound pronouncements as to our musical prowess, and a few shots of Jägermeister at the bar. We were at the height of our tour, and the night was just getting started.

After the show, we were invited to a party at the Hollywood Roosevelt, and it was a true movie moment come to life. Jake and Bruce Willis shared a cigarette by the pool. I shot a round of pool with Kid Rock, who said, "Just call me Bob," and then I spotted Mark Cuban, who had just launched the first high-definition TV station called HDTV. Empowered by the magic of the moment, I sauntered over and introduced myself, telling him we just played a showcase on Sunset and had a music video that would be AMAZING on HDTV. This was before *Shark Tank*, but he was already a billionaire and well-known for selling Broadcast.com at the height of the dot-com bubble. He said to get in touch with his office on Monday and send over the music video and that he'd get it on air, "provided it doesn't suck." Well, a few days later, I did just that, and, true to his word, we got the music video for our hit single "Home" on HDTV!

From Hollywood we headed over to Malibu the next day and performed in the offices of our radio promotions team. Quite a different vibe than rocking out on Sunset, but we knew it was important to show our faces and perform for the team that was working our record to hundreds of radio stations, figuring the more they knew us and loved us, the more airplay we'd get. Whether or not that afternoon performance made the difference, we eventually started getting our song "Home" onto 300-plus radio stations, and nothing beats the feeling of driving down the highway on tour, turning on the rock radio station, and hearing your song come out of the speakers. God, what a feeling that was; each time like my childhood dream coming true anew.

We played our way up to Northern California, with stops in San Luis Obispo, Santa Barbara, San Jose, and eventually playing the Red Devil Lounge in San Francisco where my family and friends came out to cheer us on. This tour held a number of completions, a number of "coming full circle" moments, where I realized that the dream I held so passionately as a teenager was, in fact, coming true each day. Sure, we weren't global rock stars like our heroes U2 or Coldplay, but we were touring the country, playing original rock music, rubbing shoulders with the who's who of the day, and signing along to our song on the radio. In those glorious, albeit fleeting, moments, nothing else mattered.

In between the highlights, there was still plenty of work, and having volunteered to take full charge of our business affairs, I had to make sure we would be able to make it all the way back to Nashville without running out of money. At the time, I calculated that it cost us about $300/day to survive on the road as a band—a meal for five at Denny's, some gas station food while filling up the tank, two rooms at a cheap hotel, and not much else. Sometimes being the business contact required nerves of steel more than performing on stage. One instance, in particular, was after playing a show in Ypsilanti, California, at big venue full of bikers and what I figured to be motorcycle gangs, I had to weave my way through a crowd of big, drunk, tattooed bikers and ask the promoter to be paid. Perhaps I was never in any real danger, but being a skinny guy with tight jeans and flared-out hair, I never felt so out of place as I did in that moment of contrast. Thankfully, we got paid and lived to play another day.

After weeks and weeks on the road, it was finally time to head home. We played shows through the Southwest on the way back in Merced, Bakersfield, Las Vegas, and Flagstaff once more before gassing up the van and taking turns driving for another 40-plus-hour marathon of Red Bull and rock radio until we arrived in Tennessee. We had a final epic show in Memphis on Beale Street to play, but first we had a 5:00 a.m. call time to perform on *Good Morning Tennessee* for a 7:00 a.m. filming. Let me tell you, waking up at 3:30 a.m. to get ready for a performance in pitch dark is not my idea of a good time. But, on the other hand, we got to perform on live TV and announce our show that evening, and that made it all well worth it. After the filming was done, it was around 10:00 a.m., and we had been up for hours. So, in congruence with the rock star lifestyle, we had some beers and visited Sun Studios where Elvis recorded, then went to a BBQ with a bunch of bikers that were also on the TV show that morning, all before winding up on Beale Street to close off our tour with a bang.

On the final drive back to Nashville, I'll always remember sitting in the back of the van, staring out the window, pinching myself at the experience we all just shared, when a thought flashed into my mind: *There's no way I'll be doing this when I'm 40... Huh?* I shook my head as if someone just poured cold water on my revelatory moment of appreciation. *Well, if I'm not doing the only thing I've ever dreamed of, what in the world* would *I do?* was the rejoining thought that answered my internal monologue. I could never have known it at the time, but that moment of unexpected introspection ultimately unlocked the next 15 years of entrepreneurial adventures.

From Harsh Krieger to Homebound

That profound question—"If I wasn't doing the only thing I ever dreamed of, what would I do?"—didn't get answered right away. Harsh Krieger continued on and eventually we did another whole tour of America just a few months after the first. But in between the two, the deal we made with the MTV production company became one of the most exciting parts of being in a band. We had licensed our whole album for use on a number of MTV shows, but they didn't give us (or anyone) advance notice before broadcasting a show with our song in it. So, even though I was never much of a TV watcher, I started watching MTV's *The Real World* and *Road Rules* religiously. Every few episodes, it would happen; I'd be watching MTV, and then—*boom*—one of our songs would come on! It was electrifying, and I'd literally jump out of my seat and start yelling, "Jake, Jake, get in here! It's on!" or just yell in general if I was home alone. All in all, 9 of the 11 songs on our album were used on different MTV shows, and it was actually one of the most profitable things that ever happened with our music. Definitely more so than playing the biker bar in Ypsilanti and asking the tattooed, mustachioed promoter for our $350.

After our second tour, after our first single "Home" was on hundreds of radio stations and nine of our songs on MTV, the album promotional cycle was winding down and we started writing music again. But somewhere around Thanksgiving 2005, a part of me realized that I wasn't as excited about going though the whole process again as I was the first time. Not only that; we would have had to raise more money and re-commit to doing everything bigger and better for the next two to three years. Somewhere in there a mélange of emotion began to arise. Just like our song's lyrics, "I'm coming home, just like before. Now I know I can afford to hold my head high...", I was ready to go back home to the San Francisco Bay Area, ready for something different and new.

After we all had a Thanksgiving break with our families, we came together as a band, sat down for a meeting, and I was a little shocked to hear what came out of my mouth: "I think we should take this opportunity to responsibly wind down our band and go our separate ways." I can't say our bassist and drummer exactly agreed, but Jake and I talked through it, and within a couple hours of deep conversation, the die was cast; the decision made. The same way it felt right to skip my ticket home from Europe. The same way it felt right to move from Europe to Nashville despite having a great life there. That's the same deep knowing that underpinned this decision. What's interesting to me is that such a big decision, with so many implications, could be made in a simple, calm way after putting in 12- to 14-hour days for what was, at that point, over three years. The divine balance of life is to play full-out, to be 100-percent all-in...until such time that it's crystal clear that that identity is falling away and it's time for something new. Honoring this deep knowing, what I now consider the authentic voice of my soul shining through with divine guidance, is indeed the hallmark of my vastly diverse career.

Within two weeks we had closed up shop. Our manager wasn't happy. Our band mates and fans didn't necessarily understand. But Jake and I were in full agreement, and I set about winding down what we had built with the same tenacity and attention I applied to building it. When it was all said and done, I was saying my goodbyes and revving up my car for another drive across the country, but this time driving solo, the same way I came. On the four-day drive from Nashville to San Francisco I had ample time to think, and on that very drive the idea for my next venture was born. Lying in bed in Oklahoma City, thinking about how many types of businesses I had learned about through running our label, the idea came to me; why not start a consultancy and work with others in the music industry as an advisor? In such a way, before I even arrived home, five years after moving out at age 18, I resolved to start Krieger Consulting Group.

Back in the Bay Area there was no shortage of hugs and requests for stories from my travels and adventures from the last half decade. It was great to be home and it felt like I had lived a couple complete lives since graduating high school and moving out. I still had long hair, wore tight clothes, and looked like a rocker. But that was soon to change as the great wheel turned and I found myself advising, at first, musicians and producers, then soon businesses from all sorts of industries. Through the band years, I had come to appreciate the creative side of business, and ultimately I came to see entrepreneurship similarly to Andy Warhol, who famously said, "Being good in business is the most fascinating kind of art." Truly, the diverse set of skills needed to turn an idea into reality, to nurture it and see it grow, to engage others and build momentum, and ultimately to create something profitable that adds value to the world is one of the most worthy challenges in life. Oh yeah, and business doesn't have to be boring; it can be just as fun as being in a band or busking in the streets.

The next year just flew by. I had moved back in with my parents, mostly with my dad and stepmom just north of San Francisco. I hustled up a few consulting gigs and started building a clientele, looking at every project as an opportunity to learn more about business while getting paid. My dad casually suggested that I should enroll in community college and that "time would fly while learning on the side," which proved to be a prescient choice later on. So, in a matter of a couple months, I had pivoted from lead guitarist in a rock band living on Music Row with our songs on MTV to living at my parent's house, going to college at night, and driving around the Bay Area consulting with whoever would have me.

I applied the same creative thinking that got us results as a record label to my consulting work. For example, I landed a project with a voice-over-IP (VoIP) company called TalkFree as a business analyst and advisor. The CEO Paul Falchi was on our band's board of advisors and helped us create our business plan a few years back. Once I had that project, I hired interns that were doing MBA and PHD programs at UC Berkeley and Stanford, dangling the carrot of getting real-world experience with a Silicon Valley tech company while they were in school. Turns out the students from top-tier universities had no issue working for me (who was taking night classes at College of Marin), and all that really mattered was that there was an interesting project they could work on that would get them class credit.

In the first half of 2006, as I asked myself, "Who am I…really?", the answer came back with nuances that didn't exist even one short year prior. Now I was a business consultant, shuttling around the Bay Area to do on-site work with client companies and hiring interns from top-tier universities while using my client projects for case studies at community college. Turns out my love of learning came to the fore and I was getting straight A's at college with what felt like minimal effort. So I leaned in further, started tutoring economics for free, and joined the student government at College of Marin. There had been a bond issued by Marin County to help modernize the campuses, and utilizing green energy was a focus that had funds behind it. This interesting confluence of events led to the next business I co-founded, Village Green Energy.

PART 2

Village Green Energy and the Dawn of Social Media

While advising on the College of Marin District Modernization Committee, looking at options to power the whole campus with clean energy, I was reaching out to Stanford and UC Berkeley students and professors to leverage their insights. This put me in touch with Mike Jackson and Robby Bearman, who had both completed a Master of Energy Engineering degree at Stanford and were consulting with energy companies, open to doing something new. Over a few weeks of getting to know each other and having them advise on the District Modernization Committee's mandate, we birthed an idea that got us all excited. The idea behind Village Green Energy was that we could source renewable energy certificates (RECs) from clean power producers and sell them to households, businesses, and schools that wanted to "go green." RECs are representations of power produced from clean sources like solar, wind farms, and biogas generators. The idea was we could buy RECs in wholesale, create a way to calculate energy consumption for our customers, then sell them RECs at a retail price, thereby allowing them to claim that they were "100% powered by renewable energy."

To this day, Village Green Energy is one of the most intellectual businesses I've been a part of, in the sense that it took a little while for others to grasp the details of what we were doing. It's also one of the only times I've really worked within a governmental framework as part of a business model. California has what's called a renewable portfolio standard (RPS), which had a target for, I believe, 33 percent of all power in California to be green/renewable by 2012. This standard was met by awarding renewable energy certificates (RECs) to clean power generators for each megawatt-hour (MWh) of energy they generated. Those certificates could be sold separate from the power itself—the electrons moving through the power grid—allowing the buyer to attribute their energy usage to a specific generator. In other words, when we calculated the power consumption of a business and sold them RECs, we would give them a sign to display that showed their business was powered by a specific solar installation, or a specific wind farm. The RECs could only be claimed once, so even though it was a little complex, it actually did work as a way to attribute green energy production to consumption.

Mike, Robby, and I worked on Village Green Energy out of their third-floor unit in an old Victorian house in the Castro district of San Francisco. On lunch breaks or after working, we'd walk through the neighborhood. I got pretty desensitized to guys in assless chaps walking around and accustomed to the rainbow flags proudly displayed down Castro Street, essentially the West Coast capital for gay rights. Eventually, I made a friend in the neighborhood who baked pot brownies and sold them out of her house as an open-door "salon" on Thursdays and Fridays. Hanging out there I met some of the most colorful characters I've ever come across, and I appreciated getting to know the bombastic personalities of some of the flamboyant guys and drag queens who came through the "salon." It really was a who's-who of San Francisco's quirky culture back in the mid-2000s

In any event, Village Green Energy was becoming more of a focus, and Facebook had recently opened up to everyone being able to sign up for an account, not just those with a university email address. We noticed that Facebook allowed you to build your own app on their platform that could interface with their user base and leverage their growing social graph. This gave us the idea to build an app as a way to generate more business and tap into the cache of Facebook, which at the time was the hottest tech company around. So we dreamed up Green My Vino, an app where you could "gift" five minutes of green energy to your friends on Facebook. They would receive a 3D-looking coin that was displayed on their profile...and they could "go even more green" by gifting coins to their friends with the click of a button. That was how we designed the app to go viral, but we connected it with a goal of turning Napa wineries green based on how much green energy was circulated by the app. My partners, Mike and Robby, did all the calculations, and we did purchase all the RECs, so people really were giving a tiny amount of green energy to their friends. Now we needed wineries to sign on.

Well, I can tell you in truth that visiting a bunch of high-end wineries in Napa under the auspices of a business development trip was my idea of a good time. We made the rounds in Wine Country and found six or seven wineries that agreed to purchase a year's worth of green power (RECs) from us if we hit certain milestones with the app. Basically, we built the wineries into the app and got them a bunch of exposure, while users could gift more and more green energy to their friends on Facebook with just a few clicks. Once it was all set up, we launched the app and promoted to our friends. Mike and Robby got some of the Stanford fraternities to jump on board, and in less than a week, we blew our target numbers out of the water! People loved the virtuous activity of giving green power to their friends, getting the social recognition for their impact on their profile, and seeing the progress it made towards getting wineries to "go green" as well.

We went from planning and strategizing the app launch to scrambling to sign up more wineries as fast as we could, not knowing how long the hype would last. I think we ultimately got 12 or more wineries to purchase a year's worth of RECs from us in just a couple weeks, and it impressed upon me how social media was unlocking new realms of potential online. The dot-com boom and bust of 2000/2001 had given way to a new crop of tech companies that were commanding massive valuations, and Facebook was one of the fastest-growing of them all. It's funny to think that pitching Facebook for a Campus Invasion Tour back in 2004 didn't get traction, but now we didn't need their approval and were just using the platform to drive Village Green Energy into prominence, garnering some great media mentions and new opportunities for us in the process.

Village Green Energy did over $100,000 in gross revenue in our first year in business, which was fun to be a part of, but ultimately Mike and Robby wanted to take their careers in different directions, and I was about to do the same. What I realized from consulting and co-founding a tech company was that pretty much every company needed to raise money at some point. Even if the founders underwrote the start-up costs, somewhere along the line capital was needed to hire a team, do product development, run marketing campaigns, and grow. So, while doing Village Green Energy by day, community college by night, and an occasional consulting gig here and there, I started to put feelers out for how to find investors and connect them with businesses raising capital. This led me to meet the CEO of WestCap Securities based out of Irvine, California, and kicked my post-band business life into high gear.

Initiation in The King's Chamber of The Great Pyramid

Before diving into the next phase of my career that led from green energy and consulting to investment banking and high finance, I accepted an invitation to embark on another spiritual adventure. My work in clean energy led to an interest in other forms of sustainability as well, and in the process of learning about environmentally themed design, I met a most interesting architect named Michael Rice. Michael lived in Ireland and had studied architecture at the Royal Institute of Architects in Ireland, but after his formal training his intuition led him to developing a whole new style of architecture he called biologic architecture. His style was integrating design into the surrounding land and using shapes and forms that mirrored nature instead of straight lines and more modern styles. This led to curved roofs, spiral floor plans, and expansive ceilings. He would draw entire floor plans unaided with a pencil and draft paper; his designs are a wonder to behold.

I had visited him in Ireland and toured a number of houses and buildings he designed; each one had a unique energy to it and looked unlike anything I'd ever seen. Speaking with families that lived in them, they reported more energy, healing in their relationships, and birthing gifted children, among other benefits.

Wow, what a world, I thought. Well, I had brought Michael onto a few meetings for the District Modernization Committee at College of Marin by video conference, and we were in pretty close contact. One day, he surprised me by sharing that a spiritual group in Cairo, Egypt had invited him to design a school using Biologic Architecture, and he asked if I wanted to join and develop a business model and financial plan to support his designs. I didn't have to think long and jumped at the opportunity to visit a new place with a fascinating person. But that was just the opening overture.

My father's spiritual journey had continued to develop after our Bolivia-Peru pilgrimage to Machu Picchu, and he had fallen in love with the work of a man named Drunvalo Malchizedek, who wrote a book called *The Ancient Secrets of the Flower of Life.* Drunvalo claimed to be a "walk-in"—someone who had a spiritual awakening as an adult and embodied the consciousness of an ancient mystic of sorts with esoteric knowledge to bring to humanity. His books catalyzed a global movement that grew into the millions, bringing forth ancient knowledge of civilizations from Atlantis, Lemuria, and advanced pre-historic Egypt. It just so happened that my dad signed up for a five-day, in-person workshop with Drunvalo that took place right before the trip to Egypt, and I said I'd be happy to attend, not really knowing what I was getting into.

Off we went to University of Maryland for the Drunvalo workshop; interestingly enough, the same university my father attended for over 10 years, earning three degrees. It was a homecoming of sorts for him and my first visit, and soon we were in a room with Drunvalo and 100 or so spiritual seekers, intuitives, and healers who also answered the call. From learning about ancient Egyptian knowledge, discussing the subtle energy flows at work in the Universe, and participating in hands-on healings, the workshop further opened my own spiritual awareness and intuition. In one session we did a breathing exercise, lying down with our eyes closed, and I had an experience of seeing my body as an energetic grid of light. In another session Drunvalo talked about the pit underneath the Great Pyramid in Giza where, in ancient times, initiates would descend in order to purify their fears. Spending days in complete darkness in the pit, one's deepest fears would rise to the surface, and due to the mystical energies alive in the Great Pyramid, if one's fears became too intense, they would materialize in the physical plane. The timing of the workshop leading up to traveling to Egypt myself was beyond coincidence.

After five days of bathing in mystical knowledge with Drunvalo, my dad, and the others, I boarded a flight to Cairo and was soon rendezvoused with Michael Rice on the other side of the world. There was a heavy cloud over Cairo that night when we arrived at our hotel, and I had no idea where we were, but the next morning, the sky was clear and, lo and behold, the Giza pyramids were visible just a mile or two away from the hotel looking out the window. We had breakfast and met up with the hosts who brought us out to design the school, driving to an outskirt of Cairo called El Rehab City. Our trip was five days long, but we finished just about all the work needed that first afternoon, freeing us up to explore. Of course, our first stop was the Great Pyramid!

The Great Pyramid on the Giza plateau is a wonder to behold, built from massive blocks and towering hundreds of feet overhead. Standing before it is like stepping into ancient history. Michael and I went inside and began the ascent up a very steep and narrow shaft that leads up into the heart of the pyramid. In the center of this massive structure is the King's Chamber, a room with a sarcophagus in it that is like an echo chamber in that sound reverberates off the stone walls. Magically, we were the only two people in the King's Chamber, and a mystical energy came over us standing in this ancient crypt. Michael and I stood with our backs against the walls and began to spontaneously tone, emitting a melodious harmony that was unlike anything I'd ever heard. The sounds was moving through us and out of our mouths, and we were bathed in an otherworldly choir of our own making. Time dissolved, and I felt transported back to a previous era, our voices dancing off the walls and reverberating through the chamber. It was truly an experience unlike anything I've felt before or since, and it was clear that this was the real reason why I was in Egypt.

After what could have been an hour or more, we came back to our senses and the musical intonations we were bringing forth subsided. In the dark and dull light within the chamber, Michael and I looked at each other in a stunned state of disbelief and just voiced the word "Wow" to each other in acknowledgment to what had transpired. Descending back down the shaft and out to the entrance of the pyramid, a guard at the front holding a machine gun approached us, and he didn't look very pleased. "I know what you did up there! That is not allowed! That is not permitted!" he said as my light-headed mystical state of mind quickly crashed back into this reality. Apparently, our spontaneous chamber music had wafted down to the front entrance and struck the wrong chord. "That is not allowed in here," the guard said once more, blocking our passage with the gun slung around his neck, looking more ominous by the second.

"I'm sorry. We...were just enjoying the pyramid," I said, unsure of what to say.

We stared at each other a few moments, and then the guard said, "Hmmm, well, how about you take care of me and we can forget this happened?"

Now my mind had caught up with the moment and it was clear that he wanted some cash to forgive this unknown transgression. *OK, well, that's a lot better than getting escorted to some Egyptian interrogation room*, I reasoned, and Michael and I scrambled up a bundle of Egyptian pound bank notes and pressed them into his palm. That seemed to do the trick, and the guard smiled; his entire demeanor changed. Then he continued, "Since I see you like to enjoy the pyramid, want to go down there and experience the pit?" He pointed towards a passageway with a black hole in the wall that disappeared into darkness. A full-body shiver ran down my spine, thinking back to Drunvalo's workshop and the initiates' darkest fears materializing down that lightless shaft. "Oh, no, no, that's fine, thank you. I think we've had enough pyramid experiences for the day," I managed to say, and the guard shrugged, saying that if we changed our mind and came back, he'd let us go down later on—of course, given we "took care of him" some more. The guard no longer blocking our passage, we emerged out into the bright Egyptian sun as if waking up from a mysterious dream.

In our remaining time in Cairo, we rode camels through the desert, sampled Egyptian essential oils, and viewed Tutankhamun's tomb. We sat in the central square of Cairo sipping mint tea and watching a sea of people pass by wearing hijabs as the Muslim call to prayer erupted from mosque loudspeakers at dusk. A short trip, but unforgettable; it was a continuation of the spiritual threads weaving their way through my life experience in between my burgeoning entrepreneurial adventures. When I arrived back in San Francisco, it felt like I had been gone a year, but it was less than two weeks overall.

Vice President of Investment Banking without a Degree

In the chronological unfolding of my life, this was an auspicious and heady time. In 2007, the stock market was hitting new highs every day. I'd wake up in my San Francisco apartment, cruise down to a coffee shop, and read the *Wall Street Journal*, taking note of the mergers and acquisitions between companies and following reporting on the business and financial stories of the day. One morning, after my coffee shop ritual, I drove to SFO Airport and hopped a flight to John Wayne Airport in Orange County, down in Southern California. Emerging from the short flight to sunshine and palm trees, I caught a cab to WestCap Securities' headquarters in Irvine to meet Tom, the brash young CEO that had built a multi-million-dollar investment bank in his thirties. Tom was cool, fun, loud, smart, and rich. He greeted me with a big smile, gave me a tour of the office, and introduced me to his partner and a few employees. Then, we hopped in his BMW 645ci and jetted down to Mastro's Steakhouse for our official meeting.

Leading up to this trip, we had chatted on the phone a couple times and I showcased some of my consulting clients that were looking to raise funds, and I also invested in a deal that he showed me. I was making decent money at this point for a 26 year old and figured that in investing in one of the deals his investment bank was putting together, I'd at least get an inside view to their deal structure, and at best make a nice return. Taking fast action got his attention, and I mentioned that I had a number of investor friends who might be interested in funding deals they had available too. The purpose of this meeting was to discuss me winding down consulting independently and bringing my clients into WestCap in exchange for a title and commissions on successful transactions.

I know I said that Village Green Energy was the one of the most intellectually complex business models I've been involved in, but boutique investment banking before the Great Recession was definitely another. WestCap Securities had carved out a niche in what was called the micro-cap stock space, a thinly regulated corner of the market where companies would go public on the pink sheets and small exchanges through a process called a "reverse merger." A reverse merger was where a private company was acquired by a public "shell company" that was already publicly listed but had no real operations. After the merger, the formerly private company's name became the new name of the public company and ta-da! now they were a publicly traded company! Of course, there were piles of legal documents involved in this procedure, and it was a multi-step process that involved raising money from investors just before the transaction was effected. The savviest investors knew they could sell some of their stock right when the merger was complete and make a big return, sometimes 200 to 300 percent in a few months.

Well, this was the cottage industry that WestCap specialized in, and the more I learned about it, the more intriguing it sounded, if for no other reason than it was a massive learning opportunity. I recalled my dad telling me growing up that the people who "make money using money" are some of the wealthiest around; in other words, professional investors who use their capital as a way to make money, without necessarily operating or working within any given business. Over a few-hour courtship, sipping red wine, eating Rockefeller oysters and filet mignon, we eventually got into the details of what we could do. Bottom line, I told Tom that if he gave me title of Vice President of Business Development, I'd bring all my clients to them and start actively shopping their deals to investors I knew. Oh yeah, and that WestCap would be my sponsoring broker-dealer to get my Series 7 & 63 securities licenses so I could legally get paid commissions on these type of deals.

By the time our Baked Alaska and lemon meringue desserts were a distant memory of divine flavor on our palates, we had come to an agreement and shook hands. True to his word, Tom guided me through the process of studying for my securities exams, and I got to work putting deals together. Thus began a period of manic activity that I simply loved. I'd be on the phone non-stop, sometimes eight to nine hours a day in between sending emails and studying, and oh yeah, still attending night classes at community college. The moment classes would end, I'd be right back on the phone, hustling up business and putting deals together, then reviewing business plans and merger agreements lying in bed before sleep.

One of the deals we were working on was BlueFire Ethanol, a company that claimed they could use a process called acid hydrolysis to convert plant matter into ethanol. I tapped Mike and Robby, my Village Green Energy partners with Stanford master's degrees as advisors, and soon we were sitting around a boardroom in Southern California, talking about multi-million-dollar ethanol plants, with my side of the table more than holding our own in the conversation. These conversations led to meeting a team that was building an ethanol dehydration plant in Jamaica, and since I fashioned myself as the resident renewable energy expert around WestCap, I got an all-expense paid trip to Kingston, where I soon found myself in meetings with the Minister of Energy and Technology of Jamaica, who was one degree away from the president. It's nuts thinking back on how brash and bold I was, but being in a rock band was good life experience for being confident. The difference now was instead of playing intricate guitar parts and shaking my hair around, I was talking about intricate deal points and pushing the conversations forward with everyone I met, whether that was a CEO or a government minister. Did I get nervous before some of these meetings? Sure. But I'd just take a few breaths, look in the mirror, and say, "Let's do this!" before going in, guns blazing.

This period of time set the stage for one of the main themes in my first book, *Lifestyle Entrepreneur*, which was "trading my brain for a bed." In other words, I'd take an opportunity that presented itself to travel for business deals and get the basics paid for (flights, hotels, and sometimes food). So, even though I was making decent money, I was living a lifestyle that would have cost three to four times as much if being paid for out of pocket. I saw this all as the same strand of creativity that inspired me as a musician, just with a different approach to applying that creative drive towards business and lifestyle design.

The culmination of all this deal-making was epitomized by ProVision Technology. This company invented a 3D projection technology that allowed you to interact with pictures, images, and buttons by tapping in thin air in front of one of their machines. In 2007, this was hot stuff, or so I thought, and I threw myself into understanding every aspect of the company, their technology, their competitors, and their potential. I brought the deal to WestCap, and they signed on to raise $1.5 million then do a reverse merger to become public, after which they planned to raise more money and keep growing the business. On one trip to their headquarters near Burbank, California, Tom and I had each invited some investors to come see a technology demonstration and meet the CEO. I remember regaling the investors with every technological detail of the product, talking up the potential to sell thousands of units to be placed in malls across the country and I had to catch my breath when the CEO of the company turned to me at one point and asked in earnest if he had missed anything.

Between a big investor Tom brought and a handful of investors I brought, we raised them the $1.5 million, and I was thrilled since it was my first reverse merger deal. Basically, due to securities regulations and non-disclosure agreements, the only way to see how one of these deals really worked was to have a seat at the table as part of the actual deal team putting it all together. We identified a shell company, negotiated the terms, had tons of back-and-forth with lawyers, and eventually, everything was ready to go. I got a nice chunk of stock in the newly public company that was worth around $250,000 when it started trading. The only catch was I couldn't sell it yet, and I still had to pass my securities license examinations to be able to receive the proceeds legally.

That was all the motivation I needed to study my butt off. One of the best days of my life was when I went it to sit for my securities exams. Walking in, Tom and I were on the phone, and he basically said, "Don't screw this up, or I'm keeping your commission," ribbing me and laughing like a hyena. I spent the next many hours answering questions about bond yields, options, derivatives, stock splits, and investment ethics, finally keying in the last answer. The most pregnant pause of my twenties was sitting there watching a wheel spin on the computer as it calculated my score in real time. Then, it happened—I passed! There was absolutely no talking allowed in the testing center, so I bit my lip till I got outside and promptly dropped to my knees in the middle of the financial district in downtown San Francisco yelling, "Yesssssss!!", thrusting my hands into the air like a loon. Oh yeah, then I called Tom back and told him the news. "Ohhhhh yeah, my man. Time for you to get PAID!" were his words to me.

As a result of the ProVision deal and passing my securities exams, I told him I wanted a new title: Vice President of Investment Banking. And so it was. The night classes I was still taking at community college for my degree were a walk in the park compared to the deals I was working on. "Who am I...really?" was a brash young gun living in San Francisco with a paper net worth well into the six figures and a future so bright I thought I'd need shades. As if my ego hadn't swelled to the point of explosion from all that, the cherry on top was visiting WestCap HQ in Irvine a few weeks later and Tom telling me that he was going to get a BMW M6 or maybe a Ferrari. "That sounds fun, as if you need to be able to go any faster," I told him.

Then he surprised me and said, "You've earned us all some good money this year. Here—you can ride out the rest of the lease on the 645ci," as he tossed me the keys with a dramatic flourish. I was temporarily shell shocked. Then over-the-moon ecstatic. *Holy cow! Did that just happen?* I cancelled my flight home and drove the black-on-black BMW up the California coast back to San Francisco, relishing in the glory every time I slammed the accelerator to the floor.

A Russian Romance to Discovering Project Rockstar

The next couple chapters will start to dive into an area of my life that was, for a long time, the most vexing and perhaps the most controversial; my dating life and becoming a professional dating coach. While living what felt like the high life as an investment banker, driving a $80,000 car that I didn't have to pay for, there was a growing chasm in the relationship part of my life. In high school I had a couple girlfriends, and those were enjoyable relationships. But after high school, from living in LA, Europe, Nashville, and now San Francisco, my dating life had been touch and go. I had met some wonderful women, and had a few romances while traveling, even getting into a relationship in Nashville that was great... right before winding down the band and moving halfway across the country. To be totally honest, I didn't understand women, and that was a reflection of not understanding the parts of myself that women would be attracted to.

When I was playing in bands, and especially on tour in the Harsh Krieger days, I saw the hour or so after we finished a show as my window for potential romance. If a girl was watching us play, I figured she saw me in my element, engaged in the thing I was most passionate about—music. So, it made sense that window of time after we finished playing a show was the opportune time to meet a girl. It certainly didn't help matters that we would then pack up all our gear and drive to another city. Similarly, when traveling and living in Europe, meeting girls there had the air of an exotic adventure, being outside of the normal contracts of daily life and being two people that were up for a romantic interlude that never needed to feel quite real.

Back then, I didn't understand what it meant to be a solid, grounded, masculine presence that could genuinely attract the kind of woman I'd want to be in a relationship with. I was just bouncing around, happy when something worked out and confused when something promising expired before liftoff. In spite of this, I've always enjoyed having female friends, and to this day some of my best friends are women. I value female perspectives and appreciate insight into what it's like to be a girl, let alone an attractive, amazing woman, alive in this world. I have come to appreciate that it is a vastly different experience than being a man.

Towards the end of 2007, one of my best friends was a Russian girl named Elena. We met in San Francisco. She had a wild story—she grew up in Russia and had moved to the States when she was 16, already having lived a life like girls in their 20s in America; clubbing, partying, romance, gangsters, drag racing deserted roads in Siberia, the list went on. We had been keeping in touch as I progressed from Village Green Energy to investment banking, and I had even brought her along to a couple meetings to give her some exposure to American entrepreneurship and finance. In turn, I was taking Russian language classes as part of my night courses, and it was fun to have a friend to help me access the Russian community that's alive and well in San Francisco. Elena particularly loved ProVision Technologies, and we had started dreaming up a deal where she would help sell some of their 3D projection screens into Russia and place them in shopping malls near where she grew up in Yaketerinberg. In this case, the dream progressed beyond late-night flights of fancy and became manifest.

Elena was a real go getter (she still is) and she hustled up a group of investors that agreed to buy over $100,000 worth of ProVision units. We incorporated a company in Russia, and although I didn't know the first thing about how to do that, I trusted Elena implicitly and let her take the lead. Somewhere out there is a document showing me on the Board of Directors of a Russian distributor for ProVision. Tom at WestCap was beyond amused watching this deal come together. Not only had I helped raised hundreds of thousands of dollars to take them public, but now I was striking a deal to drive six figures of business revenue for the same company, and doing it with a group of investors in Siberia. Elena came through in spades, the money was wired, and ProVision packed up a shipping container to send the units off to the distant Ural Mountains.

That is the set-up for heading over to visit Elena in Yekaterinburg over New Year's Eve going into 2008. The ProVision units had gotten held up in customs, but ever-savvy Elena had a relative that worked in customs and was able to finally free them, using some money as a lubricant to pry them loose. So, I arrived a few days before New Year's and was greeted by -20-degree weather and a warm hug from Elena. It had taken me a month to get my visa, and I was only there for a little over a week, but it was an unforgettable trip on a number of levels. First off, there was a Swedish DJ named Anders; some promoter had convinced him to come play in Siberia on New Year's Eve. The promoter neglected to say there was no hotel included in the trip and put him up at a friend of Elena's who spoke no English (or Swedish). The very day I arrived, we went over to "rescue" Anders, who had been there three days as they did drugs and partied all night. He could barely communicate with them! It didn't take long to see sparks flying between Elena and Anders in the run-up to his big New Year's Eve performance. At the same time, I met Elena's sister Anya, and while practicing my nascent Russian—and with Elena regaling her with endless stories about how cool I was, an American entrepreneur learning Russian, doing technology deals with her—sparks began to fly between us as well.

In a magical confluence of events, Elena's rescue of Anders from her friend's house had him staying with us, and just as they were falling for each other, Anya and I were getting close too. We ended up having the most insane New Year's Eve of my life. We went to an underground club, where Anders performed, and partied throughout the entire night, into the next morning, and wound up walking down the frozen streets of Yaketerinberg at 11:00 a.m. on New Year's Day, still singing and greeting everyone out and about before finally sleeping around noon. That set the tone for the rest of the week, and soon Elena and Anders were inseparable, while Anya and I were having a Russian romance in frozen Siberia. We all drove to Chelyabinsk a few nights later, where Anders performed at 2:00 a.m. in another underground club. We danced until 5:00 a.m., and then the promoter drove us back to Yaketerinberg in the frozen dawn, arriving long after sunrise, where Anya had prepared a veritable Russian feast for us and we ate like we hadn't seen food in days. One more magical memory was sitting at Anya's place, talking to each other using translate.ru to type in English, translate it to Russian, have her read it, look at me and smile, then type in Russian, translate to English, and so on, back and forth, as we got to know each other in a way that my Russian skills and her English alone couldn't allow.

Elena and Anders ended up getting married and, in a later phase in life, I loved staying with them in Stockholm, where they ultimately lived, harkening back to the most epic "How did you meet?" story that we loved to share. But, as was typical with me, shortly after leaving Russia, my romance with Anya began to fade, if only because I knew I may not be back for ages, if ever, and it just didn't seem realistic to entertain having her move to America, having known each other for such a short time. Perhaps it was the fact that Elena and Anders did have an enduring romance and wonderful relationship, or just that I had reached a tipping point where I wanted to understand more about how to actually be an attractive man, who could create a romantic partnership without needing some crazy around-the-world adventure as a backdrop.

A few Google searches sent me down a rabbit hole, winding my way through the weird world of dating advice circa 2008, but eventually yielded a real gem: A one-time-only experience for a handful of men to completely change their health, wealth, and relationship lives forever—Project Rockstar. Apparently, there was a group of guys in London who were not only in great shape and were building online businesses but had also hacked the London club scene. They had built a network of promoters, club owners, and nightlife industry folks to create unforgettable experiences and ultimately meet the kinds of girls most guys only dream of dating. The program was set to run for eight weeks out of London and required six days a week in the gym, intense seminars, and trainings in the day, then going out almost every night to work on meet girls in the top clubs in UK.

Project Rockstar was only going to accept six guys, so all their material reiterated that applications needed to be top notch. There would be multiple rounds of interviews with the instructor team, and applicants needed to be 100-percent committed for eight weeks, in person, in London, that Summer. Honestly, I had never heard of anything like this. It wasn't a paid program and it wasn't a seminar you could just sign up for, swipe a credit card, and go learn from. It was application-only and promised a full-life approach to becoming, well, a Rockstar at life.

Project Rockstar Begins in London, UK

Once I had read through the program description a dozen times and researched as much as I could about the instructor team—who all used pseudonyms but also published detailed blogs about their dating lives—I decided to apply.

"Why should you be accepted to Project Rockstar?"

"I have traveled the world, been something like an actual rock star in a band, started businesses, and even helped take a company public at age 26. I've had hit-and-miss relationships with girls in America, Europe, and even Russia, and now I want to learn what it really takes to be an exceptional man and have agency and choice in my dating life. Plus, I'll give my 100 percent and be as valuable as I can to everyone on the program, in whatever form that takes."

That was the essence of my pitch. It was actually way more detailed than that, but you get the idea. After a few weeks went by, I got a letter from one of the instructors saying I'd made the first cut and was moving on to the next round. That was all I needed to hear. I booked a 15-week return trip to Europe and invited my childhood friend Nima to join. If I did make it onto Project Rockstar, then I'd cut our travels together short and he could explore Europe on his own. If I didn't make cut for some reason, then we would still have an epic summer traveling around Europe in 2008. The economy was flashing warning signs for those paying attention, and Nima and I joked, "You say recession, but I heard vacation." I had enough money to make the summer memorable one way or another and knew there'd be plenty of time to work again on the other side of it.

We arrived in Rome and linked up with some friends of mine who were running the Colosseum Pub Crawl. They gave us a shot to be part of the team, which meant hanging out in front of the Colosseum in the day, inviting tourists to join the pub crawl, throwing frisbees around, and eating bags full of Italian dark cherries with a loaf of bread and some olive oil. Then, at 9:00 p.m., we would round up around 70 to 100 tourists on an elevated terrace fronting Via Dei Fori Imperiali, looking out over the Colosseum and Arch of Constantino, have some drinks at sunset, and then head to a string of bars. This crew had it down pat; making deals with three bars to basically close for a few hours so just our party would be their clientele. Like clockwork, each day, we brought dozens of tourists who wanted to drink and drink and dance on bars and sing along with pop songs at the tops of their lungs. Six years after hosting parties at the Haus Burgenland II youth hostel in Vienna, I was back on the streets of Europe living it up.

My application for Project Rockstar kept advancing, and then I got a message that they would like a final interview with me before deciding whether I was in or out. I got on the phone to arrange it and said, "You guys are all in London, right? Hey, I'm in town too. How about we do the interview in person?" The instructor thought it was a great idea. I hung up the phone and booked a flight to London. Although I was tempering my enthusiasm to be accepted to the program, I was also not going to leave anything up to chance now that I was already in Europe for the summer. I told Nima what was happening and took off to London.

A couple days later, I was knocking at the door of someone I knew only as Mr. M, who lived off Brick Lane near Whitechapel in London. I was expecting a tall blond guy like myself (for some unknown reason) and was greeting by a cheerful Asian-Australian guy who introduced himself as Jim and invited me in. Time became a blur as we sat in his living room; he quizzed me on entrepreneurship, living in Europe, being in a band, investment banking deals, and my goals in applying for the program. After a couple hours, he squinted at me and said, "I just can't get a thin slice on you." Let me introduce you to Braddock. He's upstairs.

I had read Braddock's blog and knew he was a total badass, oozing coolness and teaching dating bootcamps city to city, getting unbelievable reviews. Braddock asked me a bunch of questions, and I did my best to keep my composure, letting them know I'd give it my 100 percent without bragging or acting like I was a big deal at the same time. Braddock told Mr. M, "Yeah, he seems cool. I'd let him on."

I left his flat, flew back to Rome, and reunited with Nima and the Colosseum Pub Crawl—my fate hanging in the balance—shepherding throngs of tourists through the Eternal City every night. I didn't have to wait long. "Congratulations, Welcome to Project Rockstar..." was the subject line in my inbox a few days later, and I thrust my fists in the air. "Yessss!" Although I had given Nima a heads-up about this program I applied for, I'm not sure either of us really thought I'd abandon our summer travels to study the Venusian Arts with a cabal of pseudonymous dating coaches and fitness experts in London. But that's exactly what was happening, and thankfully, he understood. Well, truth is there was a little tension as I broke the news, but when I said, "If you were in my shoes, what would you do?", he didn't hesitate for a second to say he'd absolutely, 100 percent do it. We hugged goodbye, and he ended up loving traveling Europe solo, having adventure after adventure all over the continent.

I quickly adjusted my plans, flew back to London, and rented a room near Brick Lane from an ex-girlfriend of mine who I met when I lived in Vienna; she just happened to be moving out of her place in London at the same time I needed a place to live. Some divine timing at work there, no doubt. Then, Day 1 of Project Rockstar commenced, and I finally got to see what I was getting into. The instructor team welcomed us, reinforced that we had been chosen out of hundreds of qualified candidates, and then gave us the schedule; working out in the gym six days each week with an elite fitness trainer, attending four to five hours of seminar and instruction each afternoon, then going out to bars and nightclubs every evening to hone our social skills "in the field" in the truly giant and cosmopolitan City of London. We were required to journal every day and contribute to a group discussion thread on a site called The Attraction Forums. Basically, it was going to be a non-stop barrage of activities designed to explode all concepts of what a comfort zone was, breaking us down to rebuild us as elite men who could "see the matrix" and move like a ninja through all manner of social situations. Oh yeah, and no drinking on Project Rockstar. For a transformation to be real it should take place in a mindset of sober focus, not leaning on the crutch of alcohol to lubricate social interactions.

The first week was a massive change from the Colosseum Pub Crawl. I was in the gym every day, kicking my butt into shape, starting a supplement regimen, and eating healthy (but boring) food. Then getting daily downloads about the 8 Attraction Triggers, how to strike up conversations with girls and mixed groups of guys and girls and win them over quickly, and even how to meet girls in the middle of the day and go on "instant dates" to get to know them right away. Then, out we'd go to Covent Garden in the afternoon, approaching tourists and girls walking along the cobblestone streets—"Excuse me, I just saw you from over there with my friends and I'd really regret it if I didn't come over and say you look *absolutely gorgeous* today." The first time one of the instructors with a mohawk named Dr. Yen told me to run across the street and say that, I almost quit the whole program on the spot out of sheer anxious terror. But then I realized how hard I worked and planned for months and that I'd damn well better do the first exercise on Day 1 of the program that I had promised to give my 100 percent to. So, I jogged across the street, tapped her on the elbow, and told her she looked *absolutely gorgeous*.

She smiled. *Holy cow!* Then, freezing up, I said something lame like, "OK, well, have a great day!", and she shrugged as if to say, "That's it?" as I jogged back across the street and got a high-five from Dr. Yen. Then, seconds later, "Oh, mate, look at her. Go approach her. Go, go, GO!" He gave me a shove, and off I went.

Then came the nightlife. London, being the veritable crossroads of the world, has something going on every night of the week, with tourists from around the globe mixing and mingling with locals alike. Totally different vibe to approach girls in a club, surrounded by their friends with pounding music and flashing lights, then out on the street, when she may be walking home from work or on the way to a music lesson alone. The first week was pretty brutal; I got rejected time and time again in conversations with girls. Not drinking and being sore from the gym with a head full of lecture notes definitely had me overthinking, and each rejection stung, but a little less each time. For every 10 approaches that went nowhere or got a weird look from a group of girls, maybe one would work and I'd get a little further in conversation, or dance to a song for a bit before heading back to our group in the club. Being on the Colosseum Pub Crawl, where proudly had a Staff shirt on was a night-and-day difference compared with being sober in a nightclub approaching girls and groups of guys and girls more than 20 times per night. The first two weeks fried my brain and left me feeling like I was getting worse instead of better.

But then a turning-point moment came. Somewhere in the third week, after literally approaching over 500 girls in the daytime on the streets of London and then at night in bars and clubs around town, something clicked. I looked out across the sea of people in Tiger Tiger one fateful night and I "saw the matrix". I saw a group of two girls and two guys. I could see their body language; it was clear that two were a couple, and the other two were just out having fun. I saw a group of three girls standing by the bar, and it was clear two of them were trying to have fun but nursing their "third wheel" friend, who was being a downer and dampening the mood. I saw a bachelorette party on the dance floor and saw how they all deferred to one of the girls with the best dance moves, forming a semi-circle and gyrating to the beat. I saw the underlying social fabric that wove between the groups gathered and I saw my opportunity to interject myself into the action at just the right time and just the right way to sway the odds of a good encounter in my favor. I approached the two girls by the bar with the third-wheel friend. Hey, you look like the sexiest girls out and about tonight, but why's your friend being Debbie Downer?" I said, nodding my head towards the third wheel.

"What do you mean? We're the life of the party!" they said.

"Maybe you two, but not her, looking at her phone every five seconds and sucking down the vodka Red Bull like it's the answer to all life's questions," I said.

"OK, OK, you got us. She's in an argument with her stupid boyfriend, and we're trying to get her to lighten up..." And I was in! Reading the social situation like a book and inserting myself into the action was a thrill I wouldn't soon forget.

Project Rockstar Goes Next Level - Stockholm & Shanghai

With the first few bruising weeks under my belt, I started to notice a real positive change in myself at a deep level. Three-plus weeks of hitting the gym *hard*, learning tons of new seemingly secret knowledge, and becoming a social ninja while stone cold sober was building momentum. I decided to completely reinvent myself while on the program and got some new clothes and a mohawk to match my edgy new lifestyle. The daily journal entries we were all writing and publishing to the group thread were starting to get major attention in the broader dating community. One day Mr. M and I took a look at the thread, and there were tens of thousands of views, meaning thousands of people around the world were following our adventures. Then the program evolved to another level. We were required to help out on an official dating bootcamp in London that the instructor team was running. Guys paid $3,000 to spend three days and nights with the same guys we were spending weeks with. That realization put into perspective what a rare and incredible opportunity we were being afforded—spending basically the whole summer learning everything these guys knew. The next level was to go from student to teacher, or at least teacher's assistant, and elevate our own knowledge and experience by imparting it to others.

To be clear, I was out of my comfort zone every day. Project Rockstar didn't let up for a moment. But the difference between learning, implementing, making incremental progress, and teaching others felt like a big jump. One of the instructors, Jeremy Soul, invited me to Stockholm to teach a daytime dating program with him the upcoming weekend. Soon I was back in Stockholm, a city I truly love, and got to visit Elena and Anders in addition to walking the streets, pushing guys to approach flaxen-haired Scandinavian vixens in the Swedish summer sun and watching from the sidelines. Stockholm in summertime is glorious; it stays light until nearly midnight, and the weather is just divine. Each day feels like a week with the late summer sun hanging low in the sky, and Stockholm knows how to party like few other cities. Sure, I was nervous walking into the seminar room and standing at the front with Jeremy going through the theory and practicing approaches with the guys gathered around a boardroom table, but this was just the next step in my own growth. Then, out on the cobblestone streets and winding waterways of sunny Stockholm, I would get into conversations with girls myself, introduce the students to get them warmed up, then send the guys bounding across the street to introduce themselves to another group of girls.

I never would have imagined how rewarding it is to help guys get breakthroughs in this area of their lives. Sure, I had enough money to spend the summer doing this program, but I wasn't rich by any stretch. Some of the guys that signed up for the course were multi-millionaires and ran successful businesses. But the crazy thing is, the common denominator that underlies masculinity and manhood around the world is the desire to be good with women; to be an attractive man who has choice and gets to be with the girl of his dreams. The flip side of that coin—*the reason these guys signed up*—is that *not* feeling confident with women is like a gaping hole in your heart that no amount of money, prestige, fast cars, or fancy houses can fix. The truth is, so many guys work themselves to the bone to make money, thinking or hoping that somewhere along the way they'll naturally get to date the kind of girls they want. But without spending some time, energy, and attention on that goal, the money, cars, and penthouse flat downtown doesn't translate to making guys more attractive to women. At least not by default, and if girls are attracted to just the money and rich lifestyle, the guy usually ends up getting burned when the girl gets bored and finds a more attractive option, of which there are many.

These were the thoughts running through my mind when I sat down to write and reflect on the first half of the summer. Wrapping up the Stockholm workshop, Jeremy and I had become close, and we would go on to teach Daytime Dating bootcamps all over the world in the years to come. But that magical weekend in Stockholm, something new was awakened inside me. I realized that by investing this time in myself, pushing myself constantly outside my comfort zone, and building my confidence step-by-step, I was becoming the kind of guy that multi-millionaires and otherwise *truly* successful men wanted to learn from. That, in turn, built my confidence in new ways, and I poured myself into helping all the guys on the workshop get the absolute most out of it. When it came time for the attendees to leave reviews, Jesse Starlight, my new nickname, was featured in many. That worked its way back to the rest of the Project Rockstar instructor team, and I was distinguishing myself as a participant in the program. It was also an unbelievable amount of fun!

But then something happened that took things *ten thousand miles* farther than I ever could have imagined in my wildest dreams... literally.

A few days after arriving back in London from Stockholm, and we were back in the rhythm again—gym every day, seminars ever afternoon, hitting the streets in early evening, then going out until 2:00 a.m. or later in the clubs every night. Jeremy Soul had a client request a one-to-one private seminar with him. This guy, we'll call him Eskay, had recently sold his business for tens of millions of dollars and his fiancée had just decided to leave him. He said money was no object; he just wanted to finally get this part of his life solved and believed Jeremy was the guy to do it. Mr. M and I came out and met him during his multi-day one-to-one, and we all hit it off. He was suave, successful, and at a major turning point in his life. We poured ourselves into him as much as possible and also connected on a personal level, since we were all passionate about entrepreneurship and wanted to learn more about his business successes. Well, after the weekend workshop, we started getting together for dinner every couple of days. And then came the invitation that changed the course of my life.

"Guys, you've helped me loads these last few weeks, and I'm so grateful. You know, before my most recent business, I lived in Shanghai for a couple years and built a company over there. Mate, if you've never been to Shanghai, it's some next-level stuff," Eskay said, building it up big time, "so, check it out. I want to show you what life is really like in the Middle Kingdom. How about we go to Shanghai for four or five days? I'll pay for everything. It will be a blast."

Whooooaaaa. Hold the phone. What?! Yes, just like that, within a few weeks of knowing Eskay, he invited Mr. M and I on an all-expenses-paid trip to Shanghai, and with Eskay, everything was first class. Everything. So, in the midst of Project Rockstar, the lead instructor took off for five days with Eskay and me to Shanghai, knowing full well this was not the kind of invitation one turns down.

We flew first class on Virgin Atlantic, with a private bar in the front of the plane, full reclining seats, and delicious food—the works. First class on the magnetic levitating bullet train from the airport to the city center, then a massive suite at Hyatt on the Bund looking over the famous skyline of Shanghai. We checked in, showered up, and I had to pinch myself more than once to believe what was happening. The 2008 Olympics were underway in Beijing, and Shanghai was decked out with Olympic regalia everywhere, the city of 20-plus million a bustling megatropolis of activity. Eskay, our Mandarin-speaking British host, unlocked the city's mysteries one after another. Dinner our first night there was a reunion of 10 of his entrepreneurial friends seated at a large round table with rotating center plate, where a choreographed team of waiters placed baijiu liquor, hot pot delicacies, wonton treats, and a bunch of dishes I couldn't pronounce the names of. Shot after shot, story after story, the Middle Kingdom came into focus and the unescapable realization dawned on me: *THIS* is where the action is.

From our marathon, three-plus-hour dinner, I felt welcomed, a warm kinship with so many people I just met. Eskay did us a great service by telling everyone how much of a positive impact we had on his life in such a short time. The net worth of that dinner table was well into the nine figures, essentially none of which was contributed by yours truly, but it further underscored how valuable a skill it is to be able to instill confidence in a man with regards to the opposite sex. These were roughly the thoughts floating through my mind as we were whisked over to the Bund riverfront nightlife district and up into Bar Rouge, overlooking the Pudong River and epic skyscrapers, including the tallest building in the world on the other side. After refining my social skills sober for weeks, then starting to teach and help other guys, having a few drinks in me was like rocket fuel, and I wasted no time talking to half the girls in the club. Eskay and Mr. M were loving it. Hell, I was loving it! It was like a dream to be halfway around the world from London, literally the last place I ever imagined being in summer 2008 when I took off for Rome from San Francisco weeks earlier.

The sights, the smells of China, the back alleys with bamboo scaffolding stretching up 20 floors into the sky, the laundry drying outside windows, flapping in the breeze. The indecipherable Chinese characters, the fast-talking taxi drivers, grunting, wearing tank tops rolled up over their stomachs, cigarettes hanging off their lower lips. The vicious burn of baijiu liquor, followed by the flavorful explosion of a dumpling and mouthful of noodles. The glowing skyline stretching as far as the eye can see in every direction. The sleepless nights and sunrise views walking back along the Bund. Eskay showed us what life is like in spectacular Shanghai and, in between all the action, shared insights about the business culture and expat opportunities in the Wild, Wild East. This all made a searing impression in my fertile mind, planting seeds that would grow into a lush garden of opportunity. I couldn't have known it at the time, but this trip catalyzed a massive shift in my life. Over the next five years, I started a USB flash drive business that manufactured in China, studied Mandarin Chinese at UC Berkeley,

Beijing Normal University, and National Taiwan University, and so much more. But for a few magical days out of time, we were guests of a true legend, learning more about Eskay's charmed life as he rolled out the red carpet and gave us an unforgettable experience for which I'm eternally grateful.

And then, the red carpet rolled back up as our time in China wound down. Back on the mag-lev train, back to the Virgin Atlantic first-class cabin, back to Heathrow Airport, and pinching myself once more as I walked down Brick Lane less than a week later to my little room on the border of a Bangladeshi neighborhood in London to complete the final two weeks of Project Rockstar.

Going Supernova and the Glorious Future

What can I say about the final days of Project Rockstar? The fact is that this summer felt like an absolute lifetime in and of itself, taking me from the Colosseum Pub Crawl in Rome to the high-end nightlife of London, to Stockholm, the City of Bright Light Nights, and all the way to Shanghai. In the process I went from being an eager student of social dynamics to a veritable instructor in the making. Considering that guys paid $3,000 for a three-day weekend intensive, eight weeks was like 20 back-to-back bootcamps with no downtime in between. But what's more is I made friends with an amazing network of international entrepreneurs and all-around amazing men. I came to appreciate that there are certain friendships that form by convenience or default, like growing up together or being in school. Then there are friendships that form on the basis of mutual interests, passions, life goals, ambitions, and the pursuit of excellence. On the final weekend of Project Rockstar, the instructor-student divide had completely disintegrated (on purpose), and we became friends, brothers in arms, guys dedicated to living full throttle and taking ownership of our desires in life, getting after it with a fire inside. We called this "going supernova"; when all areas of life are firing on all cylinders, it creates an explosive effect that is both very attractive to others and attracts all sorts of amazing opportunities.

The last night before we all disbanded, we got bottle service in a big club in Essex, danced around for hours, drinking together for almost the first time, and jumping around on the club couches with our arms around each other, having the time of our lives. In what became a running theme in my life for many years to come, I made plans to reunite and help out on a weekend bootcamp coming up in a month or so. That way it wasn't "Goodbye"; it was simply "See you soon!" But it was also clear that the whole group of us had done some truly special and that we would never be together in the way were right now, at the end of eight weeks on an experimental one-time-only opportunity to learn from the best, and become the best in the process. Yes, the marketing for Project Rockstar very much emphasized that this was a one-time-only experience. But by the last night, it was clear that the instructor team and yours truly didn't want to see it end. Not to get too far ahead of myself here, but it did not end that misty late summer evening in Essex, England. Oh no, it went on to run for over a decade to come, and my life became inextricably intertwined with the legendary group of guys that put this together, eventually becoming a key part of the program for over a half a decade.

But that was all in the distant future, and after hugs and "I love you's" all around, I prepared to fly back to the States. In my back pocket was in invitation Eskay made to a British friend, whom he'd helped start a USB flash drive business. I met with the guy, Johan, who was running it, and over a couple coffees we made a handshake deal that if I built my own customer-facing brand in

America, we could share manufacturing infrastructure in China and get lower costs by placing larger orders together. Eskay, the legend that he is, even offered to lend me £40,000 to get it off the ground. Before I headed to Europe that summer, I had moved out of my swank apartment in the North Beach district of San Francisco, so I arrived home to my parents' spare bedroom and a warm hug, and a thousand questions. Pretty sure I slept two solid days after getting home from the accumulated exhaustion of the last three months and especially final few epic weeks. When my brain was finally back in the right time zone, I marveled at the experience I just had. I told Tom at WestCap all about it. He told me he felt the change and that the only thing cooler than being a VP of Investment Banking is being a CEO. That little offhand remark solidified what had been brewing in my mind since arriving back; that it was time to launch my own business and build a company I could run from anywhere in the world, if only so I could continue having adventures with the Rockstar crew around the globe.

My motivation was on a whole other level. I knew it was up to me to take everything I learned over the summer, all the relationships formed and opportunities unearthed, and build a new life for myself so it wasn't all just a flash in the pan. My dad graciously invited me to hang out and live with them for a while and loved this exciting new person I was becoming. So, I made the decision to accept Eskay's offer and Johan's partnership opportunity and got to work fast as lightning. I discovered an online talent platform called Elance (now Upwork) and hired a graphic designer and web developer. I did a bunch of research on whole USB flash drive industry in the States and discovered was that almost every company that sold promotional USB flash drives did so as part of a broad array of other products, like ceramic mugs, stuffed teddy bears, etc. When I looked into it deeper, I discovered that out of the 100-plus styles of flash drives most companies offered, there were only a small handful of very popular styles. I contacted all the companies, posed as a customer and politely pumped them for information. "Yeah, I'm lookin' at putting in an order for 1,000 flash drives for my community college. Yeah, I'm on student government, and we're doing a big enrollment push. What's the most popular style you guys have. What do people really love?" It only took a few days of this to narrow down nine styles of USB flash drives that comprised over 80 percent of all sales. The crazy thing was there was one style in particular, the USB Twister, that made up 80 percent of sales among those top nine styles.

With this research in-hand and the manufacturing side in-place, I choose the name USB Superstore as the brand name. The irony is that we only carried nine different styles of flash drives, but I thought it sounded snazzy and USBsuperstore.com was available, so I snatched it up, gave the web developer a brief, and got to work. I invited a good friend of mine, Rachel, to be a co-founder and shortly thereafter invited a guy I knew from high school who was great at sales to join us. Since I brought the whole business ready to go, I offered them each 10 percent of the company and a modest base salary, then a percentage of sales whenever they closed a deal. In less than two months, we had a website set-up, an ad campaign running, driving traffic to our site, and a form for customers to submit indicating what style of flash drive they were looking for, what color, what logo/branding on it, and whether they wanted us to pre-load information onto the flash drives. We were a one-stop-shop for corporations, colleges, and eventually even government agencies that were buying anywhere from 250 to 10,000-plus flash drives per order. The beauty of this business model was we would only need 5 to 10 customers per month to make it really sing.

Every morning and evening I'd sit in my dad's big red recliner sofa chair, put my laptop on top of a cushion and work, work, work, getting it all set up. I was back in classes at College of Marin and getting straight A's with what felt like minimal effort. I have always loved learning, and I'm grateful that I started classes right after my band days, since I was now getting close to being able to apply to transfer to UC Berkeley and complete an undergraduate degree at a top-tier school, but there was still a few months before applications were due. USB Superstore did pretty good out of the gate; we had a secret advantage, though, as I could back-channel any questions to Johan, and we'd share strategies, as his business, doing the same thing as I was, was performing well in the UK and Europe. Then we had three factories in South China that we would shop each order to and get the best pricing possible. The set-up I put in place was to have USB Superstore tape printed up, then the factories would complete the order, give us a visual inspection with pictures and occasional video calls, then box it up, put USB Superstore tape all over the box, and ship it direct to the end customer. In short, it was a drop-ship business, but with wholesale orders of a standardized product that was customized for each client with their logo, boxes, and pre-loaded data on the drives.

Business grew into the five figures of monthly revenue within the first couple months of launching. Soon, we got a little office in Sausalito, right on the waterfront, looking across the Bay to San Francisco, and worked out of there. I was learning tons about running ads and SEO (search engine optimization), and soon our website was getting ranked so high that we barely had to advertise. I actually documented the details of this business pretty extensively in *Lifestyle Entrepreneur*, so feel free to dive into the details there if this kind of business model appeals to you. For me, at the time, this was the next step of my dream coming true. In the first 12 months in business we made just under $500,000 of gross sales and had around a 25 percent net profit margin on that. But most importantly, I could throw my laptop in a backpack, grab my suitcase that somehow was never fully unpacked, and head off on adventures. One weekend it was helping out on a dating bootcamp in Chicago, then New York, then Miami. A few weeks later, I'd fly to Hong Kong, take the train over the border to Shenzhen, China and visit our USB factories in person. While all that was going on, Rachel, my business partner, and I had started taking Mandarin Chinese classes in San Francisco. In this way, the unexpected trip to Shanghai began to manifest Chinese language and doing business with Chinese factories as a major part of my life for the next many years. Oh yeah, and somewhere in that mix, I realized I was attracted to Chinese girls and dated a string of them between Hong Kong and the Bay Area, practicing my nascent Chinese language skills on dates and blending this hodgepodge of dating, business, and travel interests into my own personal Supernova experience back in 2008 into 2009.

A Fork in The Road - Entrepreneur Life or Get a University Degree?

In between the continuous stream of travels and adventures, I was still living out of my dad's house in peaceful Marin County. At first it was a landing pad after three-plus months living abroad, but now I had a business doing over $30,000 a month in revenue with a team of eight people and two business partners. I bumped my two partners up to 20 percent ownership each to reflect the substantial contributions they were making. We had our office in Sausalito and occasionally would kayak along the waterfront to lunch in the downtown district, paddling alongside sea lions and waves lapping laconically on the serene waterfront. I remember this phase of life fondly and, for the most part, every day had focus and clarity; follow-up on leads, try to close deals, go on the occasional date, have dinner with my parents, attend night classes at community college, bound off for a weekend adventure with my new international crew of friends.

Ironically, within weeks of launching USB Superstore, the economy took a turn for the worse, and moving into 2009, the Great Recession had kicked off in earnest. Banks were imploding, the housing market took a nosedive, and I was watching all the stock I earned working on deals with WestCap become illiquid or drop over 80 percent in value. I had sold enough over the summer and shortly after to have made a decent net return, but all of a sudden, I didn't have a six-figure investment portfolio, and it made me double down on our efforts building the business to pivot away from the micro-cap investment industry that was taking a beat down. I remembered a conversation with Tom from WestCap from months back when he said, in effect, "The day I spend more than 50 percent of my time doing compliance with the SEC and FINRA is the day I close down shop." Well, that day had arrived. As he was inundated with souring investment business and increasing scrutiny from regulators, he did indeed close down shop, and my days as a VP of Investment Banking accordingly came to a close. In reality, I had started phasing out before I left for the summer, but it underscored the severity of what was happening across the economy as a whole when the high-flying securities business I was a part of ceased to exist.

While this was all happening, I was coming to a fork in the road. I had been attending community college for over two years, using my entrepreneurial undertakings as the basis for my business and economics class projects, largely maintaining a 4.0 GPA with what felt like a marginal effort. Now it was time to apply to transfer into a university to finish my undergraduate degree. I was really only interested in transferring to Stanford or UC Berkeley, and so I carved out time to create compelling applications for each. This gave me time to reflect on everything I had done since driving across the country from Nashville and leaving the life of a rock musician and indie record label owner, through to a consultant, investment banker, and now CEO of a location-independent online business, growing each month even while the economy tipped into recession. *What is it that drives me? Who am I...really?* I asked myself anew as I dug deep to write applications for two top-tier universities. Eventually, I completed the applications with an essay on Project Rockstar and how I passionately pursued a course of personal growth and development, even if it meant doing some of the most unconventional things imaginable. Finally, I took a deep breath, smiled, and hit submit.

For the following many weeks I largely didn't think about my applications and leaned into growing USB Superstore, which continued to grow every month. My partners knew that I had applied to transfer, but I guess none of us really gave it much thought since I was excelling at community college without it impeding on the business at all. Rachel and I made a trip to Hong Kong and rendezvoused with Johan there, visiting a massive "sourcing fair" where there were thousands of electronics vendors, including dozens of USB manufacturers vying for our business. After making the rounds at the electronics fair, and having a few sunset drinks overlooking the epic skyline of Honk Kong, where an evening light show complete with lasers and a musical score takes place across the spires of skyscrapers on Victoria Harbor, we made a trip to South China together.

We arrived at the factories we used to produce our flash drives, and the managers had printed up a welcome sign and gave us a tour of the factory floor. Rachel and I were thrilled to see a recent order we had submitted actually being assembled while we were there visiting and took a bunch of pictures with the crew. Heading out to dinner with the managers afterwards, we had the customary shots of baijiu and some incredibly spicy Szechuan food. Johan and I toasted to the fact that we actually did build a USA flash drive business like we chatted about in London less than a year ago, and we all had a pretty fun time. By fun time, I mean we went to a 24-hour spa and got manicures, pedicures, massages, haircuts, and round after round of drinks, ultimately negotiating to sleep on the massage tables for a few hours before getting up and out at 7:00 a.m. the next morning! Those early trips to Hong Kong and China were a total riot. I still had my hair in a semi-mohawk style, and Johan and I are each around 6' 4", Rachel is pretty tall herself, and we literally towered over many of the Chinese people, who were more like 5' 3" on average. Throw in the fact that Johan speaks good Mandarin and I was beginning to get a basic grasp on it, and we were a barrel of laughs to many of the locals, who were largely amused by us and wanted us to sing Chinese songs with them, or take pictures, or both!

After a whirlwind trip to China, back in the office in Sausalito, I opened my email one day and saw a message from UC Berkeley: "Congratulations, you have been accepted!" Wow, my heart skipped a beat, and I yelled "YES!", much to the surprise of my team, who all looked at me like "What in the world is going on?!" I told them the news, and we all had a little celebration. Later that evening, after telling my parents, the enormity of what happened began to sink in. Since arriving home from Europe, building a business that had now done over $250,000 in revenue, traveling back to China a couple times, and beginning to learn Mandarin, I had been accepted to UC Berkeley, and that was the catalyst for moving out of my parents' place to live on campus. Before fully matriculating in the Fall of 2009, I was also accepted on the International Scholar Laureate Program for Business Chinese in (you guessed it) China! So, just one short year after that surprise trip to Shanghai, when I fumbled a basic "Ni Hao," I was returning as an incoming University student as part of a student group visiting Beijing, Shanghai, and Hangzhou. The scholar trip was around 10 days, and it was a rewarding way to revisit Shanghai (which I hadn't been to since the previous summer) as well as a deepening of what became a years-long relationship with the Middle Kingdom over the next half a decade.

Arriving back from China (yet again), it was time to move to Berkeley and attend student orientation. My first semester at UC Berkeley, I was 27 years old and intending to major in Political Economy and minor in Mandarin Chinese. What I knew at the time was I was grateful to have had years and years of life experience between graduating high school and attending college. What I did not know at the time was how extremely demanding Berkeley academics would be compared to College of Marin...

My first semester at Cal felt like getting hit by an 18-wheeler. Somehow, I managed getting a 4.0 at community college, being active in student government, tutoring economics pro bono, and running a growing international business. Within the first week on campus at Berkeley there literally weren't enough hours in the day to manage my course load plus run the business. Right away it was clear that I had set myself on a collision course with reality. No offense to community colleges, which are amazing places to learn, but the academic rigor of UC Berkeley felt like ten times the intensity of my previous course load. Not only that, while I had transferred in as a junior, my classmates were the cream of the crop who had graduated high school in the tops of their classes and had two years of ramping up to the rigors of Cal academics. My grades were suffering just weeks into the semester, and my business partners were rightly concerned that I wasn't giving my 100 percent to the company. It became crystal clear really quick that I had to make a choice. Either drop out of Cal, after spending two and a half years working for this opportunity and making a compelling case to be accepted over many others who would gladly have taken my spot, or somehow exit my role as CEO of USB Superstore. This is one time in my life where there really wasn't an available third option; not choosing between them meant both would suffer unacceptably, and that my health would suffer trying to work and study 16-plus hours per day.

I really gave this some thought, and honestly, it was not an easy choice. There were pros and cons on both sides. On the one hand, I made it into a top school and had the opportunity to learn from the best and brightest for the next two years, ultimately earning a degree from arguably the top public university in the world. On the other hand, I had a business earning $30,000 to $40,000 a month that still had room to grow and a team and investors that fully expected me to show up. So, I summoned all my creativity and decided to find a buyer for the business, aiming to negotiate a sale where my partners could continue to work and I could focus on completing my degree. Without telling anyone, I listed the business for sale on an online business brokerage. I found a buyer willing to pay in the tens of thousands of dollars to buy out my stake and to allow my partners to keep their roles. I thought I found the best solution possible and signed the deal. Then I told my partners and investors. The next day, three of four of them threatened to sue me to stop it from going through. Damn.

My partner and long-time friend Rachel was my one supporter in the situation. I honestly thought I found a good solution for everyone, but looking back on it, I should have included them all in the discussion instead of going through all the steps of listing the business and signing a Memorandum of Understanding with the buyer. So, while I thought my creative solution was going to alleviate the massive pressure of working and studying from sun up to sun down, the situation actually escalated much further! My first semester at UC Berkeley, I got a 2.67 GPA, definitely *not* the grades I was used to at community college and a far cry from my full potential. My second semester was spent giving my all in classes, then, the second I walked out the door, jumping on the phone to continue a multi-party negotiation to see if this sale could actually go through. Talk about stress. This this was (and remains) one of the most stressful times of my entire life. So many times it could have gone either way. I knew that if negotiations broke down, I could wind up in multiple lawsuits and perhaps have to drop out of school just to deal with all that, or I could reach some kind of consensus and manage transitioning myself out with some semblance of grace.

Finally, after weeks of negotiations, studying my butt off, and pulling a full course load at Berkeley, a light appeared at the end of the tunnel. My partner that had been holding out and our investors agreed to the sale with a number of conditions for how they would be involved after it closed. I was able to consummate the sale with the buyer, who, bless his heart, remained interested and actively supportive of the deal while I ran around trying to hammer out all the details. Then, once the sale actually took place, I spent the next month plus change training the new owner to operate the business and transitioning all the different levers for control over to him. While all this was taking place, I was studying Mandarin Chinese with a passion and had applied for a study abroad program in Beijing for the Summer of 2010. My goal was unequivocally to complete the sale and fully extricate myself from all operations at USB Superstore before the plane took off to Beijing.

As the semester drew to a close, my grades were improving. I got a handle on the rigors of academic life, and in a characteristic flourish fit for a book, I got it all done. Signed, sealed, and delivered. The new owner was happy, my partners satisfied, investors on board with the deal, and I was free! I can still see it clearly now, looking out the window as my plane departed San Francisco for Shanghai, this time turning the page on the business I built after my first fateful trip there two years earlier. This time, I was far from a rookie first timer gawking at life in China as a tourist. This time, I was staying in Shanghai for two weeks with a good friend Mark before starting a summer language intensive at Beijing Normal University as a UC Berkeley study abroad student. This time, I felt something waiting for me on the other side when the plane touched down. This time, I knew the experience I just had was worth writing about. This time, it would be more than a travel journal. This time, while in transit from the end of one journey to the beginning of the next, a new idea was born: It was time to write a book!

The Early Days of *Lifestyle Entrepreneur* from the Forbidden City

Shanghai in summer of 2010. So good to see you again! The Bund waterfront district lights illuminating off the river. The welcoming smile of a Chinese girl I met my first day in China two years ago, and who I saw last summer on the scholar laureate program, glad to have me back. My good friend Mark opening up his condo to me for two weeks, catching up over Szechuan chili chicken and Tsingtaos. My Chinese language skills slowly progressing but still struggling in the vast world of Mandarin intricacies of the Far East. The sticky sunshine and chirping birds in eternal contrast to the honking horns and bustling life of this truly massive ancient city. Notably absent from this increasingly familiar picture was any remnants from the business I had built and sold over the prior 18 months. In this case, the timing worked like a charm, and I had the whole summer to look forward to, first in Shanghai, then in Beijing.

After the first day or two of catching up with friends and adjusting to the drastic time zone difference, I sat down at a desk on the 34th floor of a condominium tower in central Shanghai, opened a new document, and started typing. At the time, my thought process went something like this: *I just built a business from the ground up that did close to $700,000 of revenue in the first 18 months and sold it. There will never be a time when the experience is so fresh as it is right now. I should document what it really took, how I built the systems, and my strategy in doing so, and I should write it in a way where someone else could follow the steps to build a location-independent business of their own.* So, I dove right into the meat of it. I documented how the website was built and how I chose the product selection. I wrote the progression of running paid ads to learn what customers were searching for, and then used that data to optimize the keywords on our website so we began showing up organically (i.e., free traffic) in search results. I detailed the operational model that brought a customer from the Internet at large to our site, how they requested information, how we presented options to the customer, and ultimately, how we finalized the sale and put it into production, following it through to a tracking number when the order shipped to the customer from China with our branded stickers all over the box.

For 10 days I got lost in the sauce. Mark had gone out of town, so I had his place to myself. I woke up, did some exercise, drank a smoothie, and kept writing. At the time I never really intended it to be a personal story but rather a how-to guide for entrepreneurs that wanted an online business they could run while traveling the world. Or, if not traveling the world, at least structuring it in a way where it didn't matter *where* they were. For all the products we sold at USB Superstore, none of them ever filtered through our office in Sausalito. It was all end-to-end, from factory to customer. We had even got it to the point where we weren't paying for any web traffic at all (no advertising), and the value of the leads arriving in our inbox every day was in the thousands of dollars of potential business.

That was a big reason why the company could be sold. Someone else just had to learn the ropes, reply to the leads, price out their order, and submit it to the same manufacturers we had always used. Nowadays it's become more popular to have a "drop-ship" business or an Amazon products business, but in 2008, when we started it, this was a newer concept, and I didn't see too many instructional resources available for creating a similar type of business. Overall, it was fun and therapeutic to write after months of wrangling through negotiations and finally freeing myself to focus on academics.

Then it was off to Beijing to start my summer abroad! Walking through the Forbidden City, sitting on flimsy plastic chairs in the narrow Hutong alleys lining the city center. Watching old men in tank tops suck snails out of shells while playing mahjong and chain-smoking cigarettes. There is something unique about the capital of China and its denizens relative to the sprawling cities in the rest of the country. China is less of a country than it is a civilization. Beijing has roots stretching back thousands of years and countless dynasties, emperors, and eras. Now I was moving in to Langui Gongyu apartments near the West Gate of Beijing Normal University tucked in between the 2nd and 3rd Ring Roads. I had applied for study abroad grants and basically had the summer paid for except for a few minor expenses. It began to dawn on me that for the first time in almost 10 years, I wasn't running a business. My only responsibility for the next two months, and then for the next two years, was to study, learn, build relationships with teachers and classmates, and fully embrace the student lifestyle. Sitting in meditation at the Summer Palace at the feet of a giant Buddha, looking over the lake that was the playground for emperors across the years, I opened myself to this new phase of life and committed to make the absolute most of it.

In the first week of classes I saw an opportunity. There were four different levels of classes we could test into, and the placement test was exceptionally hard. I barely understood half of the Chinese characters on the test despite having completed two full semesters of Chinese at UC Berkeley. Beijing Normal University is where Chinese teachers come to study in order to become professional teachers, and it is considered the most prestigious school in China for this reason. I had tested into Level 1, the easiest of the four levels available. After the first week, I started to get my bearings a little more. Studying, speaking, writing, and reading Chinese four hours every day in class, then working on one to two hours of homework was a massive acceleration from one hour per day of class plus homework at Cal. But I saw this as an opportunity to triple down on my studies, and one of the teachers told me that if I completed Level 3 or 4 classes in Beijing, I could skip an entire *year* of Chinese back at Berkeley. So, I went and talked to the administrator and asked if I could take Level 3 classes even though I didn't test into them. I basically said, "Give me a shot. If I'm not making the grades, I'll go back to Level 1." Then I promptly hired a Chinese language tutor to work with me an hour every day. I was amazed to learn that the tutor I hired was the first girl in her entire village to go to college, and she wouldn't accept more than the equivalent of five dollars per hour to tutor me.

The way I saw it, now that I had completed the sale of my business, I was the CEO of my college career and my top objective was getting a great education and learning everything I could with the time I had. Oh yeah, and getting straight A's was part of that objective. So, every day after classes, I sat with my tutor, made sure I understood everything, had her review my homework and assignments and give me suggestions and feedback before turning them in, and wouldn't you know it, my grades began to soar. While in Level 3 classes, within two weeks, I was getting A's on quizzes and even got a number of A+ grades on my written assignments. By the end of the summer I saved all the papers I wrote in Chinese that got an A+ and took a picture of them all together. That was something I was (and am) truly proud of achieving.

Outside of class, we all still had plenty of free time to explore the city. From Tiananmen Square and the Forbidden City to the Summer Palace and Chaoyang Park, everything was new and historic and fun to explore. The study abroad program also had some cool activities planned for us too. One Friday afternoon, we all loaded onto an overnight train to Hohhot, formerly known as Kweisui, the capital of Inner Mongolia in the north of mainland China. Twelve hours of rattling along the tracks overnight, laughing, drinking baijiu, talking with locals, and finally catching a few hours of sleep. We explored the Mongolian desert, rode camels through the Gobi desert, and slept in yurts on the Mongolian steppes, out in the grasslands a thousand miles from the dense urban life in Beijing. It was like stepping back in time to the age of Genghis Khan, and all the signs and menus were in a mix of Chinese characters and Mongolian vertical script. Such a mind-bindingly foreign mix with practically nothing in English. Yet, slowly but surely, Mandarin Chinese was coming into focus as I learned more and more of the tens of thousands of pictographic characters that comprise the language.

On another weekend trip we went to a section of the Great Wall of China where you could hike up past where it had been renovated. We climbed for what felt like an eternity, up nearly vertical steps and winding stretches of the wall until we reached a section that was like 1,000 years old, trees growing out of the center walkway, ancient stonework intertwined with roots and plants. Looking out from the perilous perches on the Great Wall, it was the Mongolians they were defending against. I learned that not only does the Great Wall of China extend over 13,170 miles but that the beginning is called Old Dragon's Head (Qinhuangdao Shi), such that China itself is enveloped by a massive stone dragon. These were my day-to-day experiences in the summer of 2010, and when the summer was winding down, it felt like another miniature lifetime had elapsed. At the closing event, a group of students and I put together a musical performance, and I played guitar while everyone sang the popular song "Dui Mian de Nu Hai Kan Guo Lai." After collecting my degree and taking a picture with my teachers, who were well pleased with the progress I made, I had a "Twilight Zone" moment, thinking how never in a million years would I have pictured myself playing guitar and singing in Chinese in Beijing when we were touring the country in a rock band living in Nashville. And yet, just five short years later, that's how my life had evolved, embracing each moment's majesty and being equally amused and surprised with the situations I found myself in.

The Only Time in My Adult Life I Haven't Run a Business

After the summer study abroad program ended in Beijing, I flew back to Shanghai for another week before heading home. This time I had two different expat clients who wanted me to run private dating seminars for them. The timing worked out, and I was going to make a couple thousand dollars from it, so I figured why not end the Summer in China back in the place where it all started just two years prior—Shanghai. I arrived and purposely had booked the same hotel I stayed in on that first trip, the Hyatt on the Bund. I had signed up for a Hyatt credit card and had some status points, so I got free club lounge access, which meant two meals a day of delicious food and a nice place to write in my off time. In between studying Chinese, scaling the Great Wall, and riding camels in the Gobi desert, I was slowly chipping away at what would become the chapters for my first book. I was purposefully writing in a variety of places, which formed what I thought was a cool undertone to the book; that it is not only about building an online business you can run from anywhere in the world and leveraging Chinese manufacturing for a global client base, but that

I actually wrote a good part of it on the ground in China, from the Northernmost province of Inner Mongolia to the bustling Southern manufacturing hubs of Shenzhen and Guangzhou. I was starting to feel as though this was my second home.

When I had an appointment with a client, I'd close my laptop, meet him in the room looking out over the Bund, and teach him everything I could about meeting and attracting the kind of women he really wanted to date. Then we'd descend upon the city, starting the evening at Bar Rouge overlooking Pudong, where I would help him meet as many women as I could. I would demonstrate how to approach a girl, make a connection, get her laughing, and move towards the potential for intimacy, which the clients always want to see—one of the reasons they pay thousands of dollars for the experience. Personally, I enjoyed the high-pressure situation—someone who paid a lot of money observing my every move as I worked the room and made connections with groups of girls and guys out at the clubs. Then I would watch with laser eyes as the he would try to do the same and make mental notes to break down every aspect of the interaction for him later—body posture, hand gestures, what he was actually saying, and the reaction of the girls he would talk to. Sometimes I'd even go chat with the girl afterwards and get *her* opinion on what he did well (or not), of course without telling her I was coaching him through the evening. That all became valuable feedback for the next day when we met up and debriefed the evening, before I taught him even more and we'd do it all again that night.

Quite a different experience to having been a student, living in a student dorm on campus in Beijing, hiring a daily tutor and studying Chinese with a passion...to staying in a suite in Shanghai with guys paying thousands of dollars to have me play James Bond with them out at the top nightclubs. When I was in Beijing, I largely turned that side of me off and no one really had any idea that I had that skill set, let alone clients waiting for me in Shanghai after our study abroad program completed. But other than that week of working with a couple guys, I really was a full-time student, and when I arrived back at Berkeley for fall semester, it was a whole different ball game relative to my first year at Cal. Now I was in third-year Chinese classes, having successfully tested through an entire year of Chinese by completing Level 3 coursework in Beijing, and into advanced Political Economy studies as well. Every day I would show up with my game face on, ready to debate intricate historical political philosophies, dive deeper into the philosophical canon of works that underpins Western political thought, and attend office hours with nearly all my professors, recognizing the value of getting one-on-one time with some of the best and brightest minds in their fields.

Fall of 2010 and Spring of 2011 blended together into a thoroughly enjoyable school experience. No business to run. No stressful multi-party negotiations to attend to. Just embracing learning for learning's sake. Spending hours in the library, taking part in evening study groups, walking through campus at night, listening to the campanile bells play—that tall tower in the center of the UC Berkeley being the largest instrument in California. In between the two semesters, I switched gears and flew over to Hong Kong and Singapore to help teach two back-to-back dating bootcamps with my good friend who went by the moniker Future. We both loved Asia and were some of the first Americans to teach dating workshops in those cities. I'm sharing this because for a long time, I had kept these worlds separate and much of my work as a dating coach secret. Practically none of my classmates at Cal knew that in between each semester I would fly around the world, get put up in hotels, and be paid to teach guys how to meet and date girls. Less so did they know I had girlfriends in Hong Kong and Singapore that I would see every few months. But now let all be revealed, as my goal here to share how my life has actually unfolded and how these different identities were both all-encompassing in the moment—being a dedicated full-time student and being a respected international dating coach—but never mixed, like water and oil in the same canister of life, amorphously swirling around each other with their own fluid dynamics.

As fun as it was to bound off around the world in between semesters, I thoroughly enjoyed being a full-time student. To this day it remains the only time in my adult life I haven't been in some stage of starting and running businesses. In place of the entrepreneurial responsibilities of product creation, hiring and managing people, marketing and selling products and services, and scaling up was my new day-to-day of attending classes, actively participating, reading 100 pages a day of material, completing assignments, student study groups, and office hours. On the occasional moments that I had free time, I'd chip away at the manuscript for my first book. At the time, the working title was *The Entrepreneur's Guidebook*, and it was a step-by-step guide to building a physical products-based business that leveraged manufacturing in China to fulfill a global client base. Specifically, it was about how to structure a business like that which could be run and managed anywhere in the world with a laptop and internet connection. I didn't know exactly when I'd finish it, but I had been chipping away at it since landing in Shanghai in the summer of 2010.

As the spring 2011 semester was coming to a close, I was technically supposed to graduate, but I did some research and saw that

I could petition to extend one more semester and then graduate in fall 2011. That would allow me to complete a minor in Chinese Language and Culture, a goal that was now within reach having tested through a whole year of coursework during my summer in Beijing. As my petition was accepted, I quickly realized that meant I had another summer before graduating in fall. So, I decided to make the absolute most of my time at Cal and applied for a business Chinese study abroad program at National Taiwan University in Taipei for summer 2011. Within a week or two, I had the rest of my year lined up; Taiwan in the Summer for more Chinese, then finish strong with one last semester on campus at UC Berkeley. I was 29 years old and absolutely loving learning all day every day.

Taiwan Swan Song and Finishing Strong

This time when the wheels lifted off at SFO Airport, I had my eyes on the prize: Enjoy another summer abroad learning Chinese and get wind up with three degrees by the time I graduated. I had my degree from Beijing Normal University, now I'd add National Taiwan University, then the capstone of UC Berkeley. First I co-led another dating workshop in Hong Kong and Singapore with my man Future. By summer of 2011, I literally felt like I had built a second life in Asia. This was something like my tenth trip across the Pacific in three years, and now I had whole friend groups in Hong Kong and Singapore that I got to see every few months. No more visiting factories in South China; instead, just having fun teaching another group of guys their way around a woman's mind and how to become a more attractive appealing man...then hitting the nightlife, talking to every girl in sight and leaning back against the bar, sipping a drink, watching two to three students at a time interact with groups of girls in the club. Now that I could "see the matrix," it was like life with cheat codes; whenever I saw a student starting to lose interest with the girls he was talking to, I'd bound over, put my arm around him, and say, "Whaaat's up, bro! Yo, are these girls cool, or are they trying to take advantage of you?" Then I'd look the girls up and down like "Stay back. This one's mine," or say something silly like that to reignite the energy and bring some fun and laughter into the conversation. One of the biggest mistakes guys make is trying to be all serious when they're out at a nightclub, where there's music blasting, people drinking, and everyone wants to have fun. One of the main things I taught guys was to match, and slightly exceed, the energy level of the girls they were talking too. Bring the fun, BE the fun, and invite them into your world, instead of seeking, searching, probing to see whether the girls can bring some fun into yours.

After two more wild weeks of epic Asian adventures in Hong Kong and Singapore, it was time to switch gears to student mode and take my Chinese language skills to the next level. Summer of 2011 in Taiwan was a scorcher! Every day felt like 90 percent humidity, and the second I'd walk outside the student dorm or classroom, I was drenched in sweat. The moment I got home, the first thing I'd do was jump in the shower to cool down then lay under the AC for 10 minutes so my body would stop threatening to overheat. National Taiwan University campus has a beautiful palm-tree-lined street leading up to the library, and I bought a bike on campus for around $75 and rode it to and from classes every day. But after class was over, I'd drop my books at the dorm, grab some dumplings from a street vendor in a plastic baggie with vinegar and hot sauce poured in it, and go explore. The great thing about Taipei is there is a massive network of bike paths that run all over the city and along the Danshui river that winds its way through the capital to the Taiwan Strait. Even better, there are tsunami walls that separate the river from the city, so once you're on the bike paths along the Danshui, it's like entering a nature preserve with bountiful trees, egrets flying over reeds, and boats cruising up and down the waters.

In Taipei I fell in love with cycling on a whole new level. Riding along the river one way, I'd wind up leaving the city and cycling through rolling hills and small towns, ending up in Wulai with epic tropical-tree-lined cliffs, hot springs, and a waterfall. Riding along the river the other way, I'd trace the curves of the Danshui to Duchuantou Old Town district, grab a snack from the street vendors, then go a little further to marvel at the wide-open Taiwan Strait, just 100 miles away from Fuzhou on mainland China but a world away. Taiwan felt like living on a tropical island, and the experience was made special by the excellent Chinese language teachers I had, with whom I never spoke a word of English. In Taiwan they use traditional Chinese characters, which are quite a bit more complex than the simplified characters used on mainland China. It was definitely an increase in difficulty over all the Chinese I had studied thus far, but a suitable next step, given how much I was investing into learning the language. This summer I made quite a bit of progress on the manuscript, getting close to having written 150 pages of content by the time I left Taiwan.

By the end of the sticky hot summer in Taiwan, our student group wrote and performed a 30-minute drama for the regular students and school administrators. I was pleasantly surprised that we could write a multi-part play and act it all out in Chinese. Quite a far cry from choking on tones, trying to say the simplest of phrases just three years prior. Then the summer was over; another amazing experience in Asia, courtesy of UC Berkeley's generous study abroad program that covered most of the costs. Back in California and back on campus once more, there was the impending sense of finality with each class, quiz, and exam. I was now in fourth-year-level Chinese, taking the most advanced political economy courses available, and I even joined the Cal Cycling Team for my last semester. That love of cycling that blossomed in Taiwan extended to team rides through the Berkeley hills, across the East Bay, and ultimately included a 100-kilometer ride from San Francisco down the coast to Santa Cruz. Such a contrast from my first semester, struggling to keep up with the coursework and feeling torn between running a business and being a full-time student.

After moving back to the Bay Area from Nashville and taking my dad's advice to "just start taking college courses because time will fly and it will be over before you know it," that time was close to arriving. First on the sidelines of co-founding Village Green Energy and becoming a VP of Investment Banking while at community college, I had matriculated to a university student and was on track to graduate the day before I turned 30. In that final semester I started to look beyond life on campus and think about what my next career move would be after graduation. I completed a first draft of the manuscript for *The Entrepreneur's Guidebook* and hired a designer to build a website for a new business idea called China-USA Traders. I figured that I would use the book I wrote to get a few consulting clients and let that be my transition into whatever would become my next full-time venture. Graduation Day was everything I had dreamed it would be, walking down the aisle with my cap and gown, shaking the chancellor's hand while receiving my diploma, and tossing my cap in the air with thousands of freshly minted UC Berkeley alums. My parents and childhood friends joined, and we spent the afternoon walking through campus and dining at The Claremont Hotel. For the sake of posterity, I will share here that in my final semester I managed to get straight A's. My mom and dad were so proud. I shed a tear in partial disbelief that I had matured from the guy who skipped class at high school to play guitar to getting top grades at a top school and that I loved the person I had become. Ten years later, whenever I'm back in the Bay Area, I still go walk through campus, sit on the ledge under the campanile looking out across the bay to the Golden Gate Bridge, and think back to the wonderful times I had as a student at UC Berkeley. Fiat Lux and Go Bears!

PART 3

Lifestyle Entrepreneur Comes Alive

It was a fitting display of synchronicity that I graduated on December 18, 2011—the day before I turned 30. Fitting in the sense that it neatly wrapped up my twenties and all the experiences that wild and magical decade contained with a bow. Synchronicity in the sense that my entrepreneurial wheels were starting to roll again, and now a number of simultaneous aspects of my identity burst forth, unconstrained by semester schedules, study groups, and student life. Carrying on what felt like a time-honored tradition, I had two dating bootcamps lined up to teach in Singapore and Hong Kong with Future just after school ended. I remember well that the first thing I did after completing my last final was go lay on the grass near the campanile and call him to coordinate the logistics and lock in my flights. This time in Singapore we taught the seminar portion of the bootcamp in the Temesek Club, a lush private estate for Signaporean Military officer members. One of the locals who had helped us out on bootcamps over the years was a local guy named Marcus Ho. We had become close over the course of sharing these bootcamp experiences; deep personal development and breakthrough knowledge in the classroom followed by fast-paced action and the real sense that anything could happen each night we hit the clubs.

Over lunch one of these days in Singapore, Marcus told me his book on Facebook ads was just published. My curiosity immediately piqued, I asked him how the experience was, and he said it was great; his publisher was super supportive, got his book in major bookstores, and helped him set up promotions and speaking opportunities. I told him I recently completed a draft manuscript for a book on entrepreneurship and asked if he would connect me with his publisher. "Absolutely, brother. One hundred percent!" was his response. Just like that, I got introduced to the CEO of Kanyin Publications based in Kuala Lumpur, Malaysia. They published a number of English language books as well as Chinese titles, and from what Marcus shared, they sounded like the perfect partner to help me turn my eBook into a proper published and distributed book. I had built a new consultancy called China-USA Traders and was using the eBook version of *The Entrepreneur's Guidebook* I wrote as a front-end incentive to win consulting clients. I marketed the book online and then had invitations to contact me if the reader wanted hands-on support to build a business that manufactured in China and sold physical products to customers around the world. Marcus got excited by the idea too and connected me with Adrian Kok, the founder, that very same day.

Adrian got back to me and invited me up to meet and explore the idea together in Kuala Lumpur. Now that I wasn't in a rush to get back to the States and start classes again, I simply said, "Yes, let's do it" and booked a bus ticket for a few days later. Singapore is a sovereign city-state at the tip of the Malaysian peninsula, and there is a bridge that crosses over a strait and into Malaysia proper.

After an epic bootcamp weekend where I wound up singing Guns N' Roses karaoke at the top of my lungs at 4:00 a.m. among other unleashed festivities, I boarded a bus, crossed the border checkpoint, and smiled at how quickly my life was getting interesting right after graduation. Winding up Malaysia from southern Johor Bahru, past Malacca, and eventually into the modern metropolis of Kuala Lumpur, I checked into a hotel right near the twin Petronas Towers in the center of town and spent the first night walking through the tropical jungle-esque cityscape. I marveled at the mix of women in hijabs as well as Western styles, Chinese people mixed with darker-skinned Malays, and a handful of expats; it appeared to be a cultural melting pot. Before meeting with Kanyin Publications, I did a little homework, visiting four or five bookstores around the city and looking for Marcus' book. I was pleased to not only find it face-out on the shelves in most stores but also to see that Kanyin had dedicated wall space to display their latest titles, which were mostly business and self-help-type books. That impressed me enough to decide I would do pretty much whatever was required to sign with Kanyin to publish my book.

The next day I met with Adrian Kok and his chief editor Carol Lin over coffee and I had a printed-out version of my manuscript that we looked at together as we talked. Adrian is a fun guy, a total ball of energy. "What's up, bro! Marcus says you're working on a book that I gotta check out. Dude, you speak Chinese? Ha! This is great!" I couldn't tell if he was always this enthusiastic or if I was getting special treatment from Marcus' introduction, but he seemed genuine and constantly had a big smile on his face, so I just rolled with it. Carol was a little more introspective and thoughtfully reviewed my manuscript while Adrian and I talked. I told him how Asia was like my second home; that this was close to my fifteenth trip but my first time in Malaysia. Adrian, of Chinese heritage, loved the fact that I am a tall white American who speaks Chinese and actually knows a thing or two about Chinese language and culture (one of the three languages in Malaysia). After a couple hours of getting to know each other, and on the tail-end of a weekend seminar teaching guys to "take ownership of your passions and go after what you want in life," I took my own advice and went for it. "Adrian, Carol, you both seem really nice, and Marcus has fantastic things to say about you. I visited a bunch of bookstores and saw your books everywhere. What do I need to do for you to publish mine?"

Adrian said that I checked all the boxes he was looking for and that the main thing he would want is for me to come to Malaysia and promote the book if they published it. Also, they wanted to make sure I was coachable and open to feedback, as Carol would be editing the book and would likely have a number of suggestions before calling it final and going to print. This all sounded more than fine to me, and they offered me a publishing deal on the spot. I was to get a small advance, and they would cover all the expenses of editing, printing, distribution, marketing, and promotion for the book. In turn, I agreed to come back to Malaysia at least twice to do promotional activities for the book and support it with some online marketing and promotion from my side as well. I left the manuscript I brought with them and followed up with a digital copy too, and we set a time a few weeks out to have a call and go over all of Carol's edits. We shook hands in principle, agreeing to review and sign the full publishing agreement in the near future. *Holy cow!* I was over-the-moon elated. After close to two years of writing, refining, and self-publishing a digital version online, I had one epic meeting with a popular business publisher in Malaysia and got offered a publishing deal!

On the bus ride back to Singapore, my mind went into overdrive. *So, in a few weeks, I'll get Carol's edits, then I'll need some time to do rewrites. If everything stays on track, we could have this book out by summer, and I could be back in Malaysia and Singapore doing a book tour before the end of the year.* I knew that the book would become the foundation for this next chapter in my life, laying out the framework for how to build a certain type of business, and that I would develop trainings, seminars, and consulting to turn it into a full-fledged business. But as excited as I was at the time, I never could have imagined how far I'd take it and what this experience would catalyze in my life that played out in epic proportions over the decade to come.

When I finally got home to the States, I saw a letter from Carol, who said she was still reviewing the manuscript and would have all her edits soon but also that after talking to me, it sounded like I had a pretty interesting life full of diverse experiences, so I should think about including some of those stories instead of it just being a business how-to book. Oh yeah, and one more thing. She suggested I change the title to *Lifestyle Entrepreneur*.

Project Rockstar Redux & Becoming a Bestselling Author

Back in the USA, I had moved out of Berkeley and back to Marin County. My dad let me use an office in an adjunct wing of his CPA practice. I got some plants, hung up a couple paintings I had picked up on my travels, and set a jade dragon from Hong Kong next to my workstation. At this stage of life, in 2012, my dad decided to make a push for getting his book/s out into the world, and I helped him find developmental writers to take some of his concepts and turn them into short-form books. In between working on edits for my book, I became adept at managing writers and churned out over a dozen of his books on topics like love, meditation, and vision statements. Interestingly enough, even though I helped bring these books to fruition with his guidance, when they were done, he pulled the plug on releasing any of them to actual readers. For 15 years now he had been giving me lectures on spirituality, the origins of mankind, and all sorts of esoteric phenomena. Now, having graduated college and putting the finishing touches on my own book, something still caused him to pull back just before the starting line. The starting line is when a book makes its debut to the world, even though that is also the completion of the writing and publishing process. At least that's how I see it, since a book can only begin to make its impact on readers writ large when it is generally available to the reading public (i.e., published).

In March I decided to fly back to Singapore and Malaysia to meet with Carol and work with her on edits for *Lifestyle Entrepreneur.* I figured it would be smart to put in some more face time with her and the Kanyin Publications team, and I decided to learn everything I could about the publishing process while going through it as an author. So, for the second time in 2012, I flew halfway around the world and arrived in the ever hot and humid tropical cityscape of Kuala Lumpur. Carol and I met for hours over coffee and various Asian delicacies like nasi lemak, roasted duck, and sticky dumplings. My book was quickly evolving from a practical, no-nonsense book on the details of launching an online business to a mix of personal stories and case studies of a handful of friends who embodied the *Lifestyle Entrepreneur* ethos that added color and context to the how-to information therein. On that trip, I got together with Adrian Kok again, and this time we had our official signing ceremony for the publishing agreement between us. We toasted espressos to the success of the book and set the joint intention that it inspire all who read it on its road to becoming a bestseller. Just before flying back to the States again, I got a most interesting invitation...

Turns out Project Rockstar grew to be more than just a "one time only" affair, and now a handful of my friends who also led dating bootcamps had banded together to run the program over summer. I had interviewed a few of them to feature in *Lifestyle Entrepreneur*, and they asked if I wanted to join them on the instructor team and lead a five-day entrepreneurship seminar, as well as work with the guys on their dating skills. The invitation included flights and hotels to Montreal, Canada for three weeks and then, after a two-week break, flights and hotels in Stockholm, Sweden for another three weeks to complete the program. Let me tell you, I didn't have to think long about that. "Yes, I'm in 100 percent. Let's do it!" was my reply. So now the rest of the year was shaping up something magical. I worked with Kanyin Publications to set the release date during the two-week break of the program and saw the most glorious summer imaginable on the horizon. That was all the motivation I needed to finish the final edits for my book and decide on the front cover design, finally arriving at a completed manuscript that was nearly ready to go to print.

The day I received the first printed copy of *Lifestyle Entrepreneur* at my office in California, wrapped in a box with Malaysia customs stamps on the outside, is a day I'll remember the rest of my life. Opening the box, holding the book in my hands, flipping through the pages, and thinking back to where it all started, writing in a condo tower in Summer 2010 after managing to sell my USB business and free myself to study in Beijing that summer. Then continuing on through to Taipei, Taiwan the following summer, where I completed the first draft. Now I had a publisher in Southeast Asia that was getting ready to publish and promote my book, and it just seemed like the perfect fit that it would be released in Asia first. The origins of *Lifestyle Entrepreneur* are intertwined with my experiences on Project Rockstar back in 2008, and now, four years later, I was on the instructor team and my book was scheduled to come out on the break in between teaching in Montreal and Stockholm. At 30 years old, with nearly a decade of entrepreneurial adventures and global travels under my belt, I felt like a new me was being birthed as the book came to fruition. There is something really special about combing through our past and culling gems of knowledge, pearls of wisdom, and stories that exemplify what's possible with the intent of inspiring and instructing the reader on how to achieve success in their life. Additionally, I was transitioning from a behind-the-scenes operator to a semi-public figure; creating videos talking about entrepreneurship, going to seminars and networking with other business owners, and creating partnerships that would help me build an audience of my own.

Summer arrived, and I hopped a flight to Montreal. Future and I shared a hotel room for three weeks, and the rest of the instructor team was just down the hall. We welcomed the students who had applied, been interviewed extensively, committed to a summer of full-life transformation, and completed a rigorous workout and diet program before setting foot in the seminar room for the first time. The seminar room was an executive suite in the Marriott Montreal overlooking the city center and a short walk to a worldly mix of nightlife and dining. I was on fire! After being super studious and excelling in school for the last two and a half years, I was unleashed, about to be a published author and swept up into the instructor ranks of the most exclusive personal development program for men in the world. Yes, that's a big statement, but show anything that rivals an eight-week immersive, where participants are screened and put through a rigorous fitness program for months before arriving to live together, learn together, go out every night together, and receive expert instruction every day. The first night out of the program is a free for all, no instruction given, just a "let's see what you've got." None of the participants were allowed to drink, but now that I was an instructor, I had a few drinks with Future as we marveled at the fact that we were teaching in a Western city for the first time. After watching the guys give it their best shot talking to girls while we were out on the town, the instructor team got a sense for where everyone was at. Then we got to work.

The program had evolved since I took part in 2008, where the seminars were held in Mr. M's living room off Brick Lane in London. Now we had an executive suite and a block of rooms in the center of Montreal with club lounge access and a program assistant to help coordinate all the logistics so we could focus on teaching and doing deep work with all the participants. But the essence and ethos were the same; take these guys from eager, ambitious beginners to social masters with entrepreneurship skills and a global network of friends by the end of eight weeks. It's amazing what kind of transformational change can take place in eight weeks of spending nearly every waking moment together, with full permission to give and receive feedback, even—and especially—if it's painful and cuts deep in the moment it's given. Outside of a school environment, I can't think of another place where grown men live together for a summer and immerse themselves in a transformative crucible of being pushed outside your comfort zone every day and night. But damn, is it fun.

In Montreal I delivered my first ever Lifestyle Entrepreneurs Academy, a five-day seminar on how to start a business that can be run from anywhere in the world based on your interests and passions. Everything I had been working on in the quiet confines of writing and editing burst out into the open as I peeled back the layers on everything I had learned starting and running businesses up to that point. I made it my personal mission to help each Rockstar identify an idea, research and refine it, then map out the specific steps and sequence of events they should take to make it real. The idea was to give each participant a personalized roadmap during the program, so that when the eight weeks was up they could pursue starting their own business and thereby not go back to their "old lives and jobs" but complete the transformation by having time and location freedom provided by entrepreneurship, plus a global network of friends to live life to the fullest. It was fun to teach, and I didn't realize how much I'd enjoy the format of helping people become entrepreneurs. I had always just been in the driver's seat of trying to create businesses myself and with partners. Now I was pivoting to being a teacher, an author, and an entrepreneurial instructor.

That was the perfect setup for what was to follow the first half of Project Rockstar 2012. In between the Montreal and Stockholm legs of the program, we had a two-week break. For the participants this was their time to travel together and deepen their bond as a group without daily instruction and going out every night. For me, it was time for *Lifestyle Entrepreneur* to make its debut in Southeast Asia! I flew from Montreal to San Francisco, washed all my clothes and had a dinner with my family, then straight back to the airport for my third trip to Singapore and Malaysia this year. I arrived back in Kuala Lumpur on a mix of adrenaline and jet lag, downed a triple espresso, and headed to the Mega BookFair taking place in the massive Petronas Towers complex in the very center of the capital. There I had more than one "pinch myself" moment as I saw my face emblazoned across banners and my book cover draped across the main showroom wall of the book fair. A group of my friends from UC Berkeley had flown in from neighboring Thailand to celebrate the occasion with me and have some fun and festivities in the capital of Malaysia.

I had arranged to fly in a friend of mine, Yaro, who is an excellent videographer, to capture the occasion. The same way that I would get flown around and put up in hotels to teach dating bootcamps,

I flew Yaro over and we shared a hotel room for my book launch with the understanding that he'd film and document the week on the ground and turn it into an epic promotional video. The stage was set. With classmates in the audience and Yaro filming, I took the stage and opened in Chinese, "Da jia hao? Nimen jintian hao buhao a?" I then interspersed Chinese into my English presentation, introducing *Lifestyle Entrepreneur,* sharing a few stories from the book, and teaching one of the main frameworks on how to intentionally craft an *identity* that is reflected in your lifestyle of choice and a business to support it. The audience gave a round of applause, and I made sure to smile at Yaro before leaving the stage to get some pre-planned promotional shots of me on stage holding my book, smiling like a loon. Then I took a seat at covered table with a big stack of my books as the Kanyin Publications team shook my hand and ushered people over to buy my book, get it personally signed, and take a picture with me.

In that span of two hours, my life changed. From being an entrepreneur, world traveler, dating coach, and student of Chinese, I added published author to the list and was surprised at how much I enjoyed meeting people, signing books, and taking pictures with those attending the book fair. Yaro had the camera rolling the whole time, and my classmates would cheer and yell in the background, "Oh my God, is that Jesse Krieger?!", shuffling people over to line up for their signed book and photo opp. The Kanyin team must have done some great pre-promotion before I arrived since it felt like people had already read my book, gotten great results, and now had the chance to meet me, but in reality, this was the big debut. After working through the line, I stood near the bookshelf that had about 50 copies of my book and big banner of me overhead and handed copies to people passing by, saying, "I think you'd love this book. Check it out." I would wait until they registered that I was the same guy on the big banner hanging over their head and smile, asking if they wanted me to sign in for them. I got a picture with the whole Kanyin Publications team and then called it a day.

The next day, my classmates and I toured Batu Caves, a massive complex tucked into a mountain on the outskirts of Kuala Lumpur, with monkeys running around outside, incense wafting out from the cave entrance, and a giant gold Murugan statue of a Hindu deity standing guard out front. Yaro was there enjoying the experience and filming, as well, to build this all into the promotional reel. Then we visited an elaborate set of waterfalls outside of town in the jungle and splashed around in the tropical heat in our swimming suits, leaving locals looking on wide eyed and smiling, a few making cat calls at the girls in the group. I filmed a short talk standing on the edge of a waterfall for Yaro to intercut into the promo video, and he edited that into a fadeaway into me speaking at a bookstore the next day. That next day, I was back under the Petronas Towers at Popular Books for an in-store reading and book signing. Yaro and the Cal crew came out again to support, and I spent a few hours meeting locals, signing books, talking about starting businesses, and even doing a few impromptu karaoke sessions in Chinese.

It was quickly dawning on me that my social skills, refined from dating bootcamps and nightclubs, could easily be converted to ways of capturing people's attention, giving them an emotional experience of meeting an author and a meaningful personal takeaway when I'd sign their book and include a nice note to them wishing them happiness and success in all they do. All throughout the store there were wall displays of *Lifestyle Entrepreneur*, and then something happened that brought me to tears. Adrian, the CEO of Kanyin Publications, showed up and said, "Guess what, bro?

Since the initial promotions went well and the book fair talk was a success, you hit number-two business bestseller!" Sure enough, inside Popular Books in Petronas Towers (the biggest bookstore in Malaysia), there was my book, sitting on the Bestsellers shelf, just behind a popular local author! That's the story of how I first became a bestselling author 10,000 miles away from where I was born and the beginning of what became my career for nearly the next decade.

When it was all said and done, that week in Malaysia was one of the funnest and most rewarding times of my life. And I didn't even mind the 15-hour flight back to San Francisco, where I washed my clothes, had dinner with my family again, then went straight back to the airport to fly to Chicago, then London, and finally arrive in Stockholm for the second leg of Project Rockstar. This time I brought copies of my book for all the participants and instructor team (some of whom are featured in the book itself). From Stockholm, after traveling literally non-stop for close to 30 hours, we boarded an overnight boat to Helsinki, Finland and sang karaoke with Scandinavian retirees and dined on the cruise ship smorgasbord buffet before taking in the scenery outside under a full moon at midnight illuminating the Baltic Sea.

To The Jungles of Borneo

The rest of summer 2012 was spent in Stockholm; it was the first summer where I was on the instructor team of Project Rockstar. I had a book out in Asia, and my long-time friend Elena now lived in Stockholm; this overlaid with my current constantly traveling group of friends. The different phases of my life had coalesced into a new identity. A new experience of life. Like an ejector seat back into entrepreneurship after two-plus years of quiet studiousness at Cal. Or rather, like the trips to Hong Kong and Singapore in between each semester, exploded out into not coming home. Or, even better, not having a fixed home and just living out of a suitcase between overseas jaunts, renting a place for a month or two at a time in Marin County as my rotating landing pad or revolving doors. The idea of Going Supernova in *Lifestyle Entrepreneur* was based on this very time, and it felt like life was a creative canvas to impress new creations upon, sharing the journey simultaneously with a growing group of people who were reading my blog and starting to read the book.

After the summer ended, I connected with the Kanyin Publications team and we started to plan a book tour across Malaysia and Singapore. The initial momentum of the release could be capitalized on by speaking at bookstores and other Mega Book Fair events around the region. I loved the idea, and we started planning my *fourth* trip to Malaysia this year. Over the next six to eight weeks, we coordinated an itinerary. Carol, my awesome editor and book confidant, offered to host me for the first leg, then her and a few of the Kanyin staff would accompany us to Johor Bahru, Malacca, Kuala Lumpur, culminating in Penang. But the part that made me happy and amused beyond all measure was starting the tour in Kuching, Sarawak on the island of Borneo! By the time November rolled around, I was off to Asia one more time. To the tropical jungles and secluded beaches on the coast of Borneo for a few nights, trading in cold, damp weather in Northern California for hot humid forests with families of wild boars dodging in and out of sight. The first place I saw my book on a bookshelf in a bookstore was in the city of Kuching, in the Sarawak province of Malaysia on the island of Borneo. I can still feel the big smile on my face, standing in a foreign land where I had never stepped foot, yet there was my book on a shelf next to some of the authors I had read, loved, and learned from over the years.

The next week was spent driving the span of the Malaysian peninsula, speaking at book fairs, meeting with the bookstore reps from Popular Books and Kinokuniya, then doing an in-store signing event after the big book fair and driving sales of the book, while fielding interest from those who had read it so far. I'd speak for an hour or so, then sign books and answer questions. These informal conversations birthed friendships, and some of the people who came had read the book and genuinely wanted to meet me and ask questions about building online businesses; others were curious to hear more about my lifestyle of seemingly perpetual travel. In between talks, Carol and the Kanyin team would take me to local eateries and laugh at me trying durian fruits and *ma po tofu* dishes. I enjoyed getting lost in the moment, staring out the window at lush rolling countryside, then arriving at an event hall with a 30-foot-tall banner of me hanging out front, then meeting a bunch of people in succession.

I felt really supported, and my first experience as a published author was becoming really enjoyable. I had included my personal email in the Introduction and Conclusion of the book and invited readers to reach out and share their story or ask questions. Through meeting people in person and getting their emails, plus people reaching out, I had built a list of around 700 people. It felt like a new variation of being in a band, but instead of a musical performance, giving a talk and doing a reading, then meeting attendees and signing books. Pack it up, get some dinner, drive to another city, and do it again. At the close of around 10 days, we toasted from a mountain top cabana in Penang to the completion of the *Lifestyle Entrepreneur* Book Tour and what Kanyin called a very positive release for *my book.*

Flying home for the holidays felt like having completed a marathon, four separate sprints across the Pacific to Asia that year, and I was in a perpetual state of time-zone adaptation. I had found a place in Madrone Canyon to rent the downstairs of a house and had something resembling a home base. I set up a white backdrop, got a camera, and started recording an audio training program to go with the book, and I started running Business In a Weekend online workshops, where people would pay $597 and join me live on video over the course of a weekend to start building the kind of business described in the book. The idea was people would read the book and then sign-up, so I offered a discount to readers. While it is fun to speak on stage and present in a one-way format, I really enjoyed working directly with people to refine their ideas and frame a business model around it. Then, what started happening is some people would reach out to my email from the Conclusion, tell me their idea, and ask if I would personally work with them one-on-one to launch it. So, I ended up signing up one or two clients a month for a $10,000 consulting package where I'd work with them for 90 days to basically implement everything in the book for them personally. By the end of three months, they would have an online business, with suppliers and fulfillment in place, and would be able to start driving sales.

Building a Business While Falling in Love

2012 was a pivotal year for me. Starting just a couple weeks after graduating Cal and turning 30, I had become a published author, traveled back and forth to Asia not once, not twice, but *four* separate times. Taught a five-day Lifestyle Entrepreneurs Academy curriculum as an instructor on the Project Rockstar program. Completed a book tour through Malaysia and Singapore. And spent weeks in Montreal and Stockholm. As New Year's Eve rolled around, I felt inspired to celebrate and some friends, and I dressed up sharp and went out to the St. Francis Hotel in Union Square, San Francisco to ring in 2013. Dressed in a red blazer, designer jeans, and a pair of stylish boots I had picked up in LA, the evening started off classy and elegant and I had a smile on my face. Then, across the room, I saw a gorgeous girl with dark hair and a sleek dress who held herself with poise and grace. Before I could get in my head and create a reason not to talk to her, I took my own advice, which incidentally I had dished out to a number of dating clients in the lobby of this very hotel. I walked over, holding eye contact, gently touched her arm just above the elbow, and said, "I saw you from over there with my friends, and I know I'd regret it if I didn't come over and say you look absolutely gorgeous."

Her look of apprehension turned to surprise, and then a smile came over her face. "Why, thank you. That is a wonderful compliment."

Still holding eye contact, now with the corner of my mouth turned up in a smile, I extended my hand and said, "My name is Jesse. Pleasure to see you..."

"Angelina," she replied and took my hand.

I gave a polite nod, still holding her eyes. "What brings you out here this fine evening, besides the obvious?"

"I am just completing a trip here, studying with a doctor, and decided to come celebrate New Year's Eve before heading back to Sweden."

"All by yourself, I see. How very bold of you."

"Why let such a small detail get in the way of wonderful evening?"

"I couldn't agree more."

We spent the evening talking, laughing, dancing, and toasting champagne. As the clock struck midnight, we were on the dance floor and in the midst of a flamenco-inspired twirl, she slipped and fell, nearly breaking her nose. Our evening of revelry took a hard left, and I escorted her to the medical station outside the ballroom. I waited with her for over an hour until the medic had assured us that there was no permanent damage, at which point I walked her back to her room. Before heading home for the night, I asked for her contact information so we could stay in touch. It was months later that I found out she normally would have given the wrong number to a guy she just met, but since I had comported myself as a gentleman, she decided to give me her real number and email.

I made it back to my little chalet in the hills of Marin by 3:00 a.m. and stood on the deck, looking out over the trees, marveling at what had just happened. Having spent so much time in bars and nightclubs, keenly observing the social fabric weaving through the sea of humanity, I could count on one hand the number of times I'd met a girl out by herself, enjoying the evening without company. I couldn't shake the thought of her. She agreed to have dinner with me a couple nights later, the evening before flying back to Sweden, and we talked for hours about travel, life, languages, and entrepreneurship. Not only was she beautiful, but she was worldly, living between Sweden and Norway, studying to be a nurse, and speaking multiple languages. Then the evening was over and I drove her back to where she was staying and wished her safe travels.

In the weeks and months to come we would write emails to each other, sharing more about our lives, sending pictures from whatever travels or adventures we were on and eagerly awaiting the other's reply. As the year was getting under way, I invested in joining my first business mastermind called Level 7 Leadership. This was a group of entrepreneurs with spiritual inclinations that signed up for a year-long journey together with the guidance of couple who facilitated the program, Brian and Jennifer. Having always felt somewhat unique relative to others who followed a more traditional career path, it was wonderful to be in the company of 25 or so creative, entrepreneurial, intelligent people sharing our experience across a number of four-day retreats spread across the year. On this program I met Michael Costuros, who was just starting Entrepreneurs Awakening, leading groups of business owners to Peru to take part in Ayahuasca ceremonies in the Andes. I also met Dane Maxwell, who had started The Foundation and was leading hundreds of people through launching software businesses, having founded a number of successful ones himself. There were a number of other wonderful people in the program, but with these two our paths would continue to cross and intertwine in some fascinating and fulfilling ways.

I was building my new business using my book as a foundation. *Lifestyle Entrepreneur* paints a picture of what is possible and gives a blueprint for how to launch an online business. The training programs, weekend seminars I was leading, and one-on-one coaching clients were how I actually made money. The economics of being an author aren't entirely lucrative on their own. If you sell thousands of books, you'll make thousands of dollars. And it is no easy task to drive thousands of book sales. But with even 1,000 people buying and reading a book, some percent of them will want further support. If even 1% of the first thousand people who bought my book wanted personal support to launch a business of their own, at $10,000 for a three-month client engagement, that is $100,000 of potential revenue...substantially more than what would be earned from book sales alone. This was how I was looking at my book and how I was evolving into the next phase of my entrepreneurial journey. No longer a behind-the-scenes operator, now I was becoming a semi-public figure, writing blog articles, delivering free trainings to partner audiences, and giving away the sample chapters from my book to build my email list and audience.

For a couple months, I shared this journey with Angelina over lengthy emails, and then a few days later would get a thorough reply and she would share how her nursing studies were going and tell me about upcoming trips she had planned. I really appreciated her thoughtfulness and elegance; to me she stood apart from so many girls I had met out at bars and nightclubs. I wanted to see where this could go, so I set the stage to see what might happen. One of my clients I was helping launch a business was a PhD in explosives science at a university in Munich. I offered to fly out and complete our final coaching sessions together in person in Germany. I had another client in Stockholm and offered him the same. Both were thrilled by the idea that the capstone of our work together could take place where they lived, in person. With that in place, I let Angelina know that I would be in her neighborhood to work with some clients and asked if she'd be free to connect. She loved the idea and asked if I had enough time to go stay at her family's cabin in Trysil, Norway for a few days. I loved that idea, and another international adventure was being born.

By the end of March, I was on a flight to Germany and arrived in the midst of winter, freezing cold but excited. Andrew Smith, who I featured in *Lifestyle Entrepreneur* and who was the lead instructor for Project Rockstar, was there, so we spent a few days exploring Munich then went to tour the explosives lab where my client Davin worked at the university. I remember him demonstrating how a certain explosive compound worked, putting some in a detonation chamber with a fork then igniting it. The fork came out gnarled and twisted with a puff of smoke, then he told us we should definitely wash our clothes before going to the airport and passing through security! Fortunately, I made it out of Germany without being suspected of carrying a bomb and arrived in Stockholm to Angelina meeting me at the gate with a hand-made sign and some flowers. My heart swooned! We drove through the frozen Swedish countryside, talking non-stop the whole way. Our letters to each other now words pouring forth from our lips. Lips that had not yet touched, but had so captivated me that I set up a trip to two different European countries just to see if she might be feeling the same. We arrived at her cabin on the outskirts of a quaint little town in Eastern Norway, and I was on my best behavior meeting her parents, with whom we'd be in close quarters for the next few days. Turns out her stepfather is an entrepreneur and one of the top nutritional supplement providers in Scandinavia. We all got along great, and that evening, stealing away from her family for a moment to look at the expanse of stars glimmering over the trees, we kissed for the very first time.

My heart was opening, and it felt amazing. For years, I had alternated between casually dating a couple girls at a time and bounding off to Hong Kong, Singapore, and other destinations to teach dating bootcamps and perhaps take a girl home from the clubs. But now, here I was, having flown halfway around the world for a girl I hadn't so much as kissed but had grown to admire and respect for her independence, drive, and lust for life. Our feelings grew, and life felt new again with her.

Throughout the rest of 2013 we would have a number of international adventures together. Each one inherently international, for it meant either I flew to Europe, she visited me in America, or we met rendezvoused somewhere else entirely. The year was a mix of working with the mastermind group, having four-day retreats once per quarter, building my business incrementally in between, and seeing Angelina somewhere in the world. By the time summer rolled around, I was once again an instructor on Project Rockstar, and this time she flew out to spend a couple weeks with me in Las Vegas where we were put up in a penthouse suite on The Strip and where I taught another Lifestyle Entrepreneurs Academy seminar. This year was markedly different, as I had a girlfriend with me, and she thoroughly enjoyed learning about this part of my life, meeting the guys that had applied and worked so hard to get onto the program, and then going out and having wild nights in Las Vegas that typically didn't end until we saw the sunrise over The Strip.

Then, just a few weeks later, we would rendezvous again in Stockholm where the second leg of Project Rockstar took place. I would work with each participant to craft their entrepreneurial ideas into business plans and action steps. Then we would head to Stureplan and party through the night, dancing, reveling in the majesty of life, and walking home alongside the waterways of Stockholm past the Royal Palace with the sunrise painting the sky. One of my readers from Estonia took a ferry over to Stockholm and was thrilled to receive a personally signed copy of my book, as well as meet a handful of the guys I featured in the book, who were also instructors on Project Rockstar. In turn, I marveled at how different this year was from the last. In fact, I don't think I went to Asia once in 2013, except for a brief visit to South Korea with Angelina and her family. But no trips to China, Hong Kong, Singapore, or Malaysia, which had been my steadfast second homes for the last four years.

Towards the end of the year, Angelina and I would talk about what our future might hold. She was a year away from finishing nursing school. I was one year into building my career as an author and entrepreneurial trainer. We went back and forth about it. She graciously offered to move to the USA to be with me but was only willing to spend up to a year there. She invited me to move to Spain where her family had bought a beautiful home near the coast. As much as the thought appealed to my world-traveling, run-a-business-from anywhere nature, I just couldn't reconcile the thought of settling down when I was still in the nascent stages of building my career. I was making some money, and had a small but passionate audience, but I knew that I would need to focus and build to realize the full potential of what I wanted to create. Angelina was about to begin her nursing career and was working with her stepfather with growing responsibilities in their nutritional supplements business. As much as we cared for each other, and as much as part of us both wanted it to work, we decided to let go and let ourselves grow each in our own direction. My final trip of 2013 was to Sweden, where we spent a few final days together and we each cried upon saying our goodbyes. It was an emotional decision and I wasn't sure if I was making the right choice, or the biggest mistake of my life.

The Second Coming of *Lifestyle Entrepreneur*

One of the other moving parts in 2013 was building my audience as an author and creating partnerships with others in the online business community. I talked a little about how I structured my offerings on the back end of the book—teaching Business in a Weekend online seminars and doing one-to-one consulting to help a few clients at a time create and launch a business of their own. At the same time, I was always looking for ways to partner with others who, in their own way, lived the principles of *Lifestyle Entrepreneur* and had an audience of their own. These were people with online businesses that taught, trained, coached, or led live events on their own particular areas of expertise. I would attend events like Brendon Burchard's Experts Academy and Marisa Murgatroyd's Live Your Message LIVE and bring a stack of books with me, signing personalized copies and gifting them to the attendees I met there. Following up on these connections, I'd offer to lead a free training for their audience, something like Lifestyle Entrepreneur Masterclass, and basically teach the topics in my book to their audience. The upshot was I got all the names and emails of people who would register for the online class and in many cases I'd get to make an offer to those on the line. If I offered an upcoming Business in a Weekend seminar for $597, then perhaps I'd share $200 per sign-up with the partner that hosted me. Or if I offered one-on-one coaching for $10,000, then I'd share $1,000.

Focusing on these types of partnerships was one of the smarter things I did in this period as I started making a name for myself in online business circles, while growing an email audience of my own. Then I'd send blog articles, free resources, and share my perspective one to two times per week with my email audience, and that, in turn, became my core group of followers that would engage with my content, refer clients to me, and, in many cases, that I'd meet with at in-person events or if I was traveling somewhere. This was a strategy I first learned from Brendon Burchard, who I thought (and continue to believe) is one of the best in the game. He masterfully shares valuable content, is personable, and also delivers tons of value in his courses and live events. In fact, it was at one of his live events where he brought his publisher on stage and did a session breaking down the strategy they used to launch his book *Millionaire Messenger* to #1 *New York Times* bestseller. I was enthralled, and it just made so much sense! The strategy came down to incentivizing people to pre-order a number of books in the weeks and months leading up to the launch by offering discounts on his live events, or giving away his online training courses for free for buying X number of books. The publisher was Rick Frishman from Morgan James Publishing, and I decided right then and there, that is who I wanted to publish the US edition of *Lifestyle Entrepreneur*.

After the event I did a bunch of research, and I saw that Morgan James Publishing was sponsoring an event in Las Vegas called Author 101 University in October of 2013. I signed up and headed out to Vegas with a friend of mine, Nick, who also taught dating bootcamps and was working on a book. I signed up for a VIP ticket, which offered the opportunity to "Pitch the Publisher," basically giving me the chance to share my book with the decision makers at Morgan James Publishing in a private catered evening part of the event. As usual, I brought a box of books with me and made connections with other attendees during the day, then before going to the VIP session in the evening, gave myself a good long look in the mirror, splashed some water on my face, and said, "Let's do this!" First, I saw the acquisitions editor for Morgan James and went up to him with a big smile, launching into my pitch: "Here, take a look at my book *Lifestyle Entrepreneur*. It was originally published in Asia last year and hit number-two business bestseller. I've built an audience of a few thousand people and would love to have Morgan James be my US publisher."

The editor Terry listened politely, nodding his head, and said, "You know what, this is exactly the kind of book we like to publish." I was elated, but just getting warmed up.

Then I saw Rick Frishman, who had spoken on stage that day and who was at Brendon's event with over 800 people. I approached him, introduced myself, handed him a copy of my book, and said, "Here, take a look at my book, *Lifestyle Entrepreneur*. It was originally published in Asia last year and hit number-two business best-seller. I've built an audience of a few thousand people and would love to have Morgan James be my US publisher."

I told him we met briefly at Brendon's event, and he nodded his head, saying, "You know what, this is exactly the kind of book we like to publish." Holy cow, 2 for 2!

Now it was time for the coup de grace, or as my Canadian friend Nick liked to say, "Go for the hat trick." So I approached David

Hancock, the CEO of Morgan James Publishing, and asked if I could have a moment of his time. He obliged, so I handed him a copy of my book, saying, "Here, take a look at my book, *Lifestyle Entrepreneur*. It was originally published in Asia last year and hit number-two business bestseller. I've built an audience of a few thousand people and would love to have Morgan James be my US publisher." Yes, literally the exact same thing I just said to Terry and Rick.

David smiled a big, friendly smile and said, "You know what, this is exactly the kind of book we like to publish."

That was all I needed to hear. I asked him to hang tight for just a second while I excitedly grabbed Terry and Rick and asked them to come over with me for a moment. When I had David, Rick, and Terry all together, I told them, "Listen, I just spoke with each of you, and each of you independently said this is the kind of book you like to publish. Well, I would love you to publish this book and I'll work my butt off to make sure it's as successful as possible."

I think they were amused, maybe even a little impressed with my moxie, and they each looked at the others with an appraising look, like, "Oh you said that too?"

Then David said to me, "Sounds like you may have yourself a deal. Let's follow up next week, and we'll send over a publishing agreement for you to review and we can take it from there."

As worked up as I had gotten myself to accost them in the VIP reception and pitch each of them my book, this floored me, and I missed a beat with my jaw hanging open. Then I smiled ear-to-ear and told them, "I'm the happiest author in all of Las Vegas tonight." We shared a little small talk and chatted amiably for a few minutes, then I excused myself. Someone wise once told me, "Don't sell when it's sold," and I didn't want to say or do anything that could detract from the perfect sequence of events that just unfolded, so I left the VIP reception, grabbing Nick on my way out, and said, "Let's go celebrate, buddy!"

True to his word, David Hancock followed up the next week and sent me a publishing agreement. They offered a modest advance and asked only that I purchase 2,000 copies of the book over the life of the agreement. Considering how fast I was going through books—giving them out at events, using them as incentives for partners, and selling them directly through my website—this seemed more than fair. Going into the holiday season of 2013, although part of me was heartbroken from ending the relationship with Angelina, I was also hopeful for the future. I got to work making some edits, updating some of the content that was Asia-specific, and taking another pass through the book, knowing it would likely be the last time I'd comb through the book word for word before sending it off for publishing in the USA, Canada, Europe, Australia, and New Zealand, essentially the English-speaking world. It was an incredible feeling to have signed two publishing deals, on two continents in two years and highly encouraging that I was joining a publishing house that helped take Brendon Burchard's book to the top of the *New York Times* bestseller list. This is my true testimony that the only two publishers I ever spoke to about *Lifestyle Entrepreneur* are the two publishers that I have signed deals with.

Going All In and Getting Committed to Building a Business in America

The last two chapters wove together the two DNA strands of my life and identity that were playing off of each other through 2013. Falling in love, traveling the world with a partner, and introducing her to the side of my life that included Project Rockstar felt like a step towards maturity and adulthood. In that process, I stopped teaching dating bootcamps and put an end to the part of my life where I got flown around the world to teach guys how to meet and attract girls in nightclubs. The other thread was my emerging author career and seeing through the Asian release of my book, onward to building a business helping aspiring entrepreneurs launch companies of their own. While one of these strands fell away when Angelina and I decided to part, the other got all my attention, and 2014 was an interesting year in this regard. While in a relationship, I had no issue living in a secluded canyon up in the hills of Marin County, knowing it was just a matter of weeks before bounding off to some new adventure. But after separating, it felt like an isolated, lonely hideaway. In short order I started to feel like I was getting "old" at the ripe old age of 32. I knew something needed to change.

One of the threads that I had carried forward from my UC Berkeley days was a friendship with a classmate named William. Midway through 2013 we had decided to try something fun and created a non-profit called University Incubator. We aligned with Kiva, a micro-lending platform where my sister worked to provide 0-percent-interest loans to student entrepreneurs with the goal of helping them "create their own job by the time they graduate." It was a fun way to stay involved with the campus community, and we funded around five student entrepreneurs leading into 2014, meeting them at Cafe Strada on the south side of campus to help mentor them and guide them towards launching their ideas into reality. So, I figured a good next step in life would be to get out of Marin and move back to Berkeley. William was up for it, and we got a student apartment on Spruce Street, a stone's throw from campus, overlooking the medieval rooftops of an artistic section of Berkeley across the street. The irony was that after having graduated, become a bestselling author, traveled the world extensively while falling in love, and signing a second publishing deal, I was now moving back into the same student apartment building I lived in years earlier when I was in school. I wanted that sense of nostalgia living near campus where so many good memories had been formed while I worked towards building my career.

It ended up being a good move, and I enjoyed morning jogs through the scenic Berkeley campus and working out of the same coffee shops where I studied a few years prior. University Incubator was a fun way to give back and help the next generation of entrepreneurs, but we both knew it wasn't going to be a full-time thing. Nevertheless, it was fun to have a project where we got to hear interesting ideas that the bright students of Berkeley were dreaming up. Interestingly enough, the one team we funded that weren't Berkeley students ended up having the most success—Moringa Connect, started by a pair of Harvard and MIT students that focused on planting moringa trees and creating products from them between Ghana and the USA. We helped fund two rounds of their early-stage financing, and I just checked up on them while writing this book, eight years later, and they're going strong. It's rewarding stories like that, which accumulate over the years, that make entrepreneurship and helping others start businesses so enjoyable.

Meanwhile, with the ink dry on my Morgan James Publishing contract for the US, UK, and Australia release of *Lifestyle Entrepreneur*, I decided it was time to double down on building an audience in the USA. Looking back, it's interesting to think that this was a real decision that I weighed for a while. At the time, I had five years of operating experience on the ground in Asia from Hong Kong and Singapore, to a book out in Malaysia, to degrees at Beijing Normal University and National Taiwan University. A part of me was making a compelling argument to build my career in Asia. But as I pulled back on international travels for a bit going into 2014, moved back to Berkeley, and connected more with American business owners and student entrepreneurs, I came to the conclusion that I should put my efforts into building a business in the good ole US of A. With that decision in place, I leaned in to building my audience, business, and brand as much as possible leading up to the US release of my book. That entailed doing online trainings, writing regular blog articles, speaking at co-working offices in San Francisco, doing online promotions with partners to grow my email list, and learning as much as I could in the process.

Of all the ways to build an audience and online business available, the one that appealed most was something called *virtual summits*. This basically entailed bringing together a group of experts on a topic, interviewing them, and giving people free access during a limited time, like for five days or a week. The idea was to get all the speakers involved to promote the event, inviting their audience to come learn for free from a number of thought leaders, and the host of a virtual summit would collect all the names and emails of the attendees. While it was free to attend, most people would offer lifetime access to the recordings plus some bonus material provided by the attendees for anywhere from $47 to $197 plus. It is a great model to get hundreds, if not thousands, of new subscribers, educate them on a topic, then drive sales all within a span of a couple weeks. As I got familiar with this model, the person doing this I admired most was Marisa Murgatroyd, who had a popular event called Superhero Summits. She would have her team create "superhero" illustrations of the participants and made it a fun, engaging way to learn and make money. I decided to take a page from her playbook and put together the Lifestyle Entrepreneur Summit to coincide with the release of my book. Instead of charging people for the recordings, I would simply ask people to buy my book and forward me the receipt to get access to all the recordings and some bonuses.

The US release date for *Lifestyle Entrepreneur* was set for June 2014 with Morgan James Publishing, so I got to work getting speakers committed to be on my summit and scheduling interviews. This was a fun time in the early stages of growing my online brand, and I was learning a ton, from web design, promotion strategy, email marketing, and constantly benchmarking what others were doing successfully. I got around 10 commitments from speakers, and most of them agreed to promote the event. I built the website myself and set it all up, wrote promotional emails for my speakers to use, and then we all started promoting it. The fun part of it was I basically got to ask people I admired detailed questions about their business strategy in the name of creating compelling content for the summit attendees. In this fashion I started to learn how people with audiences of 10,000 to over 25,000 had done it and featured their strategies as the draw to the summit. When it was all said and done, my first summit brought in about 800 new subscribers and sold a couple hundred books. That combined with all the other marketing I was doing and promoting the book to my existing audience gave a decent debut to the US edition of *Lifestyle Entrepreneur.*

What I realized in the process of releasing the book in the US was that it was more on me to handle the marketing and promotional side of things. Turns out it was a pretty special relationship with Kanyin Publications, where they took out advertisements, got me speaking gigs at big book fairs, and helped coordinate a book tour across the country. In turn, it was an amazing first experience as a published author. Now with my book out in the US, UK, Australia, and the rest of the world, it was my game to win or lose in terms of how many people actually discovered it and bought a copy. That was fine by me, as I enjoy learning by doing and I was already many months into learning book promotional strategies, implementing them, growing my audience, making partnerships, and moving things forward. I enjoyed leading in-person talks and mini events in San Francisco at co-working facilities, and I even led my first one-day Lifestyle Entrepreneurs Academy event outside of Project Rockstar. I believe 12 people showed up, plus my dad, who was my biggest cheerleader now that my book was out. My attitude was:

Anyone who shows up and wants to learn from me, I'll let it rip, I won't hold back, and I'll do my best to ensure they come away with a firm grasp of the process of starting a business or designing a new lifestyle.

The other moving part that was starting to get traction was being a guest on podcasts. I said yes to every invitation and I proactively sought out opportunities to be interviewed on the popular shows of the day. I like podcasts because they're a long format, similar to a book. In an hour-long conversation we can cover a lot of ground, go on a few tangents, dive into a strategy in detail, and basically create a valuable experience for the listener in a way that posting on social media can't. By the time I had been on over 20 podcasts of the smaller and medium variety, I eventually got the opportunity to go on *Entrepreneur On Fire* with John Lee Dumas in late 2014, which was one of the top shows at the time.

Over the previous few months I had been advising some friends that were working on books, and a few of them asked me, "Can you just do it for me?" As in, could I just handle all the publishing and promotion if they completed their book. The more this happened, the more I the idea grew on me. I had been helping people start businesses for the last couple years, and it was rewarding, but it's also such a big task to launch a business and make it successful. On the other hand, helping someone navigate the publishing process that I had been through twice and to support them with promotions on their book launch sounded really fun. So I said yes and helped Jasper Ribbers, who I had featured in my book, complete and launch a book of his own - *Get Paid For Your Pad: How to Maximize Profit from Your Airbnb Listing*. Jasper owned an apartment in Amsterdam, his home country, and was renting it out quite successfully while traveling the world 9 to 10 months each year. He had been documenting everything he did meticulously and teamed up with a co-author, Huzefa, to produce a great manuscript. We came to an agreement, and this became the first book I ever published. We had rounded up a bunch of friends from the Project Rockstar network to promote and share it, plus we had a number of other ads and partnerships that helped launch it. This was the dawn of Lifestyle Entrepreneurs Press, and that first book I published ended up selling quite well for years to come! I often thing that if that first book launch didn't go well, I likely wouldn't have pursued publishing further, but I'm glad it worked out the way it did.

Around this time I saw that Marisa Murgatroyd was getting ready to host another Superhero Summit, and I signed up for one of her courses that included a one-to-one call with her as a bonus. I was pretty nervous leading up to that call, because I promised myself that I'd ask to be on her Summit, which at the time was mostly people with seven-figure businesses that were more established and experienced. We connected well on the call, and I shared my story...then made the ask! As fate would have it, she said that someone else who was going to talk about book promotion had dropped out and there was a spot open. She told me I'd have to send at least 500 people to register for the Summit and I'd have to make an offer priced at $197 live, on-air to her audience. I told her I'd do whatever it took to send 500 people and that I'd have an amazing presentation and offer ready to go when it was Superhero Summit time. She said yes, and that was the beginning of one of my most amazing mentor relationships!

For the next many weeks I worked on creating a presentation, teaching people how to launch their book and become an Amazon bestseller in the process. I built a slide deck with over 100 slides, and I came up with an offer that I called Bestseller Campaign

Blueprint. Basically, for $197 I would teach eight weekly trainings, live, on-air with the participants, walking them through the whole process. I promoted the Summit hard, ran ads to drive sign-ups, and cleared the 500 registrations number that Marisa required. Then, Summit day arrived. Wow, I was pretty nervous going into it, and there were close to 800 people live on the line as I walked through my presentation. Then it was time to make the offer, and I walked through everything people would get for $197, reinforcing that it was *only* for people on the Summit and only good for that day and the next 48 hours. Once I got through the whole pitch, Marisa came back on the line and talked me up, adding her own marketing pizzaz and basically telling everyone it's an amazing deal to get eight weeks of live training for that price. While still on the air, I started getting sales notifications—my email started blowing up. It was an amazing feeling, something that made a big impression on me. Ultimately, over 75 people signed up for my course, netting over $13,000 of revenue from the 90-minute presentation, and best of all, I was the number-one selling presenter on the whole Superhero Summit, beating out people with much bigger audiences and businesses that perhaps didn't craft and deliver as compelling an offer as I made. Marisa *loved* it, and it became a great story that one of her students beat out the "industry leaders" that she had brought together for the event. After that all went down, Marisa reached out and invited me to her upcoming live event, Live Your Message LIVE, in Los Angeles. This was towards the end of 2014, and she said it would be a great opportunity to meet others in the online business space, plus she was going to share my story on stage.

As 2014 was coming to a close, my book had come out in the USA and I was reaching people around the world with my own message and story, plus I had published *Get Paid For Your Pad* and another book called *The Art of Resignation* on how to gracefully quit your job. At Marisa's event in LA she offered a year-long mentorship program where I would get to work with her one-to-one and as part of a small group of entrepreneurs to take what I was doing to the next level. I filled out the application even through the price tag felt like a bit of stretch. On the application, one of the questions was "If there is *one* thing you could do right now that would help grow your business faster, what would it be?" The interesting thing was that right away, my answer was "Move to Las Vegas!" I even surprised myself with that one. But at the same time, I was going to Vegas three to four times a year and had spent almost a month there each of the last three summers for Project Rockstar, where I had become a fixture on the instructor roster. Strange as it sounds, it just made sense to me to move to Las Vegas as a way to focus on building my business. I was getting bored with living in Berkeley and I had definitely outgrown the student apartment I was sharing with William. So when Marisa said she'd be happy to work out a payment plan with me for her mentorship program, I decided to make a major life change and move to Las Vegas. My plan was to build Lifestyle Entrepreneurs Press as a proper publishing company, taking everything I had learned as an author, combining it with 10 years of entrepreneurial experience, and supporting authors to launch their books and impact readers' lives.

The Dawn of the Vegas Era

There I was, 33 years on this Earth, packing up my few belongings in a Berkeley student apartment and moving them into a storage unit in Berkeley. It was February 2015, and I was moving to fabulous Las Vegas! My girlfriend at the time was hanging out with a few friends after we had brunch together on Shattuck Ave. Each trip down the stairs and into the moving van left less and less furniture, until the three of them were sitting on a couch that was the only thing left in the room. I took one more look around, standing at the window looking over the medieval wood-paneled architecture of the houses across the street and over to campus, then turned back to my girl and said, "It's time to go." We carried the couch down to the van, and I went and unloaded everything at a storage unit. The only things coming with me were my clothes, computer, a few paintings, and my jade dragon from Hong Kong. Basically, whatever fit in my BMW 325i, which wasn't very much. I kissed my girl goodbye, knowing she'd come see me in Vegas but both of us also knowing this was something of an end to our short-lived relationship. With that, I hoped in my car and hit the highway.

Two days later, I arrived in Las Vegas just as the sun was setting. It was an auspicious arrival with the epic desert sunset painting the sky a thousand colors, the Spring Mountains framing the valley, and The Strip illuminating the sky. I crashed with a friend, Richard, who I had helped mentor the previous Summer on Project Rockstar. His place in Henderson was my landing pad before I moved in with another friend, also from Rockstar, right across the street from The Strip. The excitement was palpable. The sun was shining. I set up shop in a fully furnished, two-bedroom condo on the top floor of The Meridian, which locals know as the place where professional poker players and strippers live. Trading in the gloomy winter mornings of Berkeley for the ineffable sunlight of Las Vegas, my new workspace looked out over palm trees and clear blue skies with a swimming pool and hot tub just below. Within a week I started wondering why I didn't do this sooner. In Berkeley I felt like I was getting old, living in a student apartment across the hall from where I lived years ago as an actual student. In Las Vegas, I felt like my life was starting anew. I'd wake up, hit the gym in our complex, have a smoothie, and work. Talking to authors, learning the ropes of how to do bigger, better book launches, and saying yes to every podcast and media opportunity that came my way.

After work I would bound down the stairs, cross the street, and explore every inch of all the casinos on Las Vegas Blvd. Sure, I had been to Vegas countless times, but every time it was part of an event and I barely had a free moment in between seminars, eating a meal then hitting the nightclubs with clients or friends. Now I had all the time in the world, and my childlike curiosity and wonder was at the fore. There are hidden gems in the hotels of Las Vegas. In the Mirage I found a memorabilia store that had a montage of items signed by every president in American history, all framed in one big display, and on sale for $250,000. In the Venetian I would walk alongside the indoor canal, under the interior skyline, listening to the gondoliers serenade tourists in Italian. In The Cosmopolitan I would relax after work in the middle floor of the Chandelier Bar surrounded by thousands of crystals draped around the lounge on all sides.

Just a few weeks after moving in, I was on a call with a prospective author named Rosetta, who ran a community called Happy Black Women. She told me she had a manuscript written and wanted to know how fast I could publish it and launch it on Amazon. She had an event coming up just a few weeks away with over 100 women registered and wanted her book to launch while the event was underway. I did some quick math and told her that it was possible but it would be a stretch. She told me that she'd love to have me come speak at her event and make a big event out of the book launch. She also said something that stuck with me: "Money loves speed." Essentially, she said if I could prioritize the book launch, I could come speak at her event and make an offer from stage for my Bestseller Campaign Blueprint program, which she had signed up for on Superhero Summits a few months prior. She said if I could make it all work, she'd send me $3,500 that very day. I smiled, said, "Yes, I'll make it happen," and as the money hit my account, I walked across the street to The Mirage and had a steak and Manhattan to celebrate.

Around this same time, I had put up a job post for an executive assistant. I was starting to clear over $10,000 a month from a combination of selling my training programs and signing authors for my new service, Done For You Publishing. What had started with Jasper and a few other author friends asking "Can you just do it for me?" swelled to a chorus as I wrapped up the eight-week Bestseller Campaign Blueprint training. It was a similar situation to people reaching out that had read my book asking if I could personally walk them through starting an online business of their own. But in this case, people had seen me on the Superhero Summit, signed up for my course, and then wanted to know if I'd publish their book. These were the earliest days of Lifestyle Entrepreneurs Press. For the first few books I took on and signed publishing agreements for, I simply sub-contracted the work needed and managed everything myself. But now I was ready to scale up a bit and I found a highly skilled assistant named Charlotte who just so happened to live in Atlanta; same place the Happy Black Women event was being held.

Less than two months after moving into The Meridian, I was hopping a flight to Atlanta for the event, appreciating that the airport was a mere 15 minutes from my front door. I arrived in Atlanta, checked into the Sheraton, and was pleased to see that Charlotte had coordinated all the details for my arrival and participation at the event impeccably. There were boxes of Rosetta's book waiting and order forms for me to hand out from stage so attendees could sign up for my program. Meanwhile, I had completed the publishing for Rosetta's book and had everything lined up to send a flood of traffic, buyers, and promotions to drive her book up the charts on the first full day of her event. That evening I went down and met Rosetta in person at the reception for her event. We took a picture in front of a step-and-repeat backdrop with her holding her book and me pointing at her and smiling. Then we had a R&B dance party, where I was quite literally the only white guy at the Happy Black Women event. I knew I needed to make an impression to be accepted before going on stage the next day...so I kicked off my shoes and danced for hours with some very happy black women. By the end of the night, Rosetta dubbed me an Honorary Happy Black Woman!

The next day, she invited me on stage, and I had everything ready to go. I had the audio-video team pull up Amazon on the big screen. I told them to click refresh so everyone could see this was live and not a slideshow. Then I had them put in Rosetta's name and click on her book, *Launch Your Business*. There it was, for all to see—her book was #1 Bestseller in the Starting a Business category. The room erupted in applause. Rosetta smiled from ear to ear. We got a picture on stage together, then I asked, "Would you all like to know how we made this happen? Would you like to know how your book can become a number-one bestseller too?" That was just about the best set-up for a talk on stage I could have asked for. I delivered a step-by-step breakdown of everything it took to publish a book and launch it up the charts. Then I introduced my Bestseller Campaign Blueprint program on stage, this time offering it for $997 and including some bonuses and a one-to-one call with everyone who signed up. Seventeen people signed up, and I made $16,949 in sales that day. I believe I split 30 percent of that with Rosetta for hosting me and netted $11,843 from a one-hour presentation. After the event, Rosetta took me and her team out to some amazing Southern soul food and we chatted amiably in downtown Atlanta before I hopped my flight back to Vegas. This was starting to get fun.

Back in Vegas, I leaned in harder. The more I put myself out there, the more media I did, the more successful book launches I could create, the more authors wanted to talk publishing. One of these authors was a guy named Dan Munro from New Zealand. Dan worked in the corrections department, dealing with inmates and criminals all day, and desperately wanted a change. As it turns out, he had found a copy of *Lifestyle Entrepreneur*, read it cover to cover, and started building a men's coaching business called The Brojo on the side. He reached out and asked if he could share a manuscript he had been working on. When we spoke, it struck me:

Here is someone I've never met, who lives in a place I've never been, who discovered my book, read it, took action, and now we're meeting under the auspices of exploring publishing. That call really underscored the power of a book to make a major impact in people's lives. Dan had a book called *The Legendary Life* about creating, well, a legendary life for yourself, and I told him it would be my honor to publish it.

Then I met Colin Gilmartin from New Orleans, a children's soccer coach and real estate investor who wrote a book called *Dream Training* for adolescents. Turns out he was engaged to Karol Brandt, who was working on a book with her co-author, Robby D'Angelo. Both had lost 100 pounds naturally and were in the best shape of their lives. Their book was called *The Struggle Is Real.* I signed deals with both of them and felt the momentum building weekly. Shortly before moving out of Berkeley, I had met a wonderful lady named Laura Gisborne at a joint venture partners event, where people with online businesses gathered to meet other entrepreneurs and create promotional partnerships. Laura is a nine-time entrepreneur who had built her dream home in Sedona, Arizona and was working on a manuscript called *Limitless Women.* Laura invited me to her place in Sedona for a weekend of brainstorming. As an executive coach, she offered to help me map out the future of my publishing company, and I, in turn, would help her take her book across the finish line and publish it. That weekend in Sedona she helped me crystallize a vision for how to accelerate the growth trajectory I was on and we became dear friends. She invited me to speak at her event in a couple months, and I suggested we host co-host an event for authors in New Orleans.

By the time June rolled around I was touching down in the Big Easy. Just months after moving to Vegas and getting serious about building a book publishing company, and I had already hit

Atlanta, Sedona, and now New Orleans in the name of books and business development. Laura and I booked a conference room at Hotel Monteleone, right in the heart of the French Quarter, with the famous Carousel Bar & Lounge. It was the perfect way to throw some fuel on the fire of what was percolating up in my life at the time. Moving to Vegas was liberating, and I felt five years younger upon arrival. Now co-leading an event of authors with a mentor/friend and a handful of authors whose books I was in various stages of publishing was just plain fun. We did hot seats, took a deep dive into each attendee's business, and put down a strategic plan for them to follow over the next year. All of the ideas and breakthroughs were captured on large sheets of paper, which we proceeded to hang on the walls once full. By the end of the weekend we had covered the entire conference room with the ideas, strategies, and tactics and got a picture of us smiling, surrounded by the knowledge and wisdom recorded on paper. Then we hit the town and danced to dueling pianos, had an absinthe at the Pirate Bar near the waterfront, and even got the most introverted attendee to dance on a tabletop before the night was through.

Back in Vegas, the summer was heating up, and, once again, Project Rockstar and a new class of guys descended on Las Vegas. This time, I was a local. No need to travel and stay in a hotel; I lived right across the street from The Strip and could literally walk home after a night out on the town. I had a box of *Lifestyle Entrepreneur* books delivered from Morgan James Publishing and personally signed a copy for each of the Rockstars at the culmination of teaching a week-long seminar. This was my fourth year on the instructor team, and it is always rewarding to see the alumni come back, many of whom started businesses that were conceptualized during the program. It also inspires me to see each new class come in green and grow and evolve over the summer in such a tight container of personal development and life transformation. There was always a reason why each Project Rockstar might be the last. It's a huge time commitment. The instructor group basically contributes their time and expertise for free. It is a massive planning and logistical effort. But it's also so rewarding and fulfilling that by the end of each summer, the idea to do it all again gets thrown around, and basking in the afterglow of another "summer of a lifetime," none of us can can't imagine not doing it again next year.

Not even six months into my new life in fabulous Las Vegas, and my business was growing, my place near The Strip was a revolving door of friends visiting town, and every few weeks I'd cruise 15 minutes down the street, hop a plane, and bound off to some new adventure.

Bringing Authors Together On and Off Stage

The second half of 2015 marked a quickening tempo of action and adventure. I was months into my mentorship program with Marisa Murgatroyd, who was giving me weekly insights into how to grow an exciting impactful business. I had another mentor in Laura Gisborne, who would have me on stage at her events to talk about online marketing and the book publishing process. I got the opportunity to train another group of guys on entrepreneurship during my week-long Lifestyle Entrepreneurs Academy seminar in Vegas, then we all spent three weeks in Stockholm together on the second half of Project Rockstar. Stockholm had become like a second home with a mix of friends dating back close to a decade and now four consecutive summers spent in a suite at the Sheraton with an international group of guys, getting after it just about every night, soaking up the Swedish nightlife that goes until sunrise during the summer months. When the summer wound down, I felt inspired to plan a live event for the authors I was working with and to step up my own game as a teacher and speaker.

The idea was born for Bestseller Summit LIVE, a two-day event for authors and entrepreneurs in Los Angeles. Marisa and Laura helped me plan it out and shared their strategies for negotiating with hotels to get a good package deal. I secured a room block at the Westin near LAX for November and worked with catering to plan out meals for what I expected would be around 30 people or so that attended. I invited all the authors I had published and was working with. Laura agreed to be my co-host, and we planned an award ceremony for the first night where we would present trophies to authors who had hit a number-one position on the bestseller charts with their book launch. When I told my dad what I had in the works, he got excited and booked a flight for the event, and he put the word out to some of his close friends who had been my mentors 10-plus years ago when I was in a band and starting our record label. As we got closer, I moved into a stand-alone house away from The Strip with my friends Andrew, Alex, and Swedish Alexander, whom I'd spent the last many summers with as instructors on Rockstar. There, once the event was advanced and I was sure it was going to happen, I went into hermit mode for around a month, preparing two full days of presentations and mapping out the flow for the event.

Life became simple and straightforward leading up to the event. I'd wake up, hit the gym, eat some chicken and broccoli that we had meal prepped and always available in the kitchen, then take my laptop down the street to a coffee shop. There I would labor over designing hundreds of slides for my on-stage presentations and creating the materials for the attendees. Everyone would receive a binder with worksheets in it. I also outlined a year-long mentorship program of my own that I planned to offer from stage; the name was The Author to Entrepreneur Experience. Modeling on what I saw Marisa and Laura do so well, my intention was to deliver tons of value and a fun, engaging experience in person at the event, then invite those who felt called to sign up for the year-long program, where we would implement all the plans birthed that weekend together. Honestly, it was a ton of work, and more than once I found myself getting nervous at the thought of being on stage and something going wrong or everyone in the audience having a bad experience. But what I've learned over the years is that anytime we create something new and bring it forth into the world for others to have their experience with it, that invariably brings up latent emotions, anxieties, and whatever is just under the surface that needs to be addressed. By recognizing this as a natural (and unavoidable) part of the entrepreneurial creation process, it becomes an act of courage to be present to whatever is coming up in the moment and methodically work through it.

At last, November rolled around, and I headed off to LA to lead my first live event from stage. My assistant Charlotte had helped a ton advancing the hotel rooms, coordinating the meals, preparing all the materials, and producing a step-and-repeat banner so I could get pictures with all the attendees with Bestseller Summit Live & Lifestyle Entrepreneurs Press logos in the background. Laura and I arrived a day early to set everything up, and by the time the doors opened for the attendees to come in, we had a dozen or so round tables set up with floral bouquets, binders with seminar materials, and branded pens. I would speak on the lighted stage, with a big screen set up. While I was nervous during the lead-up to the event, once the doors opened and the guest came flooding in, I was 100 percent in my element and in love with the process. For the next two days, I delivered everything I had learned about being an author, working with two different publishers, becoming a bestseller, and building a business based off the ideas in my book. In what has become a theme in my life, I used my own first-hand experience as a catalyst to explain the underlying concepts and philosophy. I think of my journey into becoming an author and ultimately a publisher as traversing a pathway into the unknown. As far as I've gone down the path, I can shine a light backwards, illuminating the steps I took and revealing the pitfalls to help others avoid them.

This approach highlights one of my main teaching points over the weekend—that everyone who feels called to write a book and *actually* does it has something valuable to share with others. Writing a book, especially a non-fiction book on business, health and wellness, or self-help and spirituality is an act of service to the reader. The reader should be able to synthesize what worked, avoid doing what doesn't work, and shave years off their learning curve when a book really delivers the goods. When a book *does* deliver the goods, then it is a natural effect for the reader to want to learn more from the author, perhaps even to work directly with him or her to accomplish similar results or heal a similar issue. Thus, a book can become your best business development tool, provided you don't hold back and use it as a teaser to try and sign clients. That's a shortcut. The real juice is in delivering all the goods in the book; delivering an entire framework, or a proven sequence of events that reliably delivers a result. When that is the case, then you have accomplished with the reader what is difficult to do in other mediums—they know, like, and trust you. So now it's not even a comparison-shopping situation between your offers and someone else who delivers similar training, coaching, or support. Now it's just about having an escalation path established so a reader can become a client and—in the best cases—get such great results that you feature them as a case study that further substantiates the quality of your ideas and authority on your subject.

In essence, that is what I mapped out at Bestseller Summit LIVE for around 35 authors and a handful of mentors who had supported me and followed my journey with amusement over the years, through all its myriad twists and turns. The award ceremony that Laura and I planned was a highlight for all. After the seminar, everyone got changed like they were going to the Grammy's, and we turned over the room so it had a red carpet leading to the stage and a table with crystal trophies engraved with the names of a handful of lucky authors. We got some amazing pictures from that evening, and the whole experience really inspired me to do more events both online and in-person. Turns out it's one of the most rewarding experiences of life to break bread and share time with those who want to learn what I am uniquely qualified to share and teach. On the final day I rolled out The Author to Entrepreneur Experience year-long mentorship program and included an application with a deposit payment to secure a spot. I believe 7 or 8 of the 35 people there signed up, and I had priced the year at around $18,000, payable monthly. Dan Munro had flown in from New Zealand; Colin, Karol, and Robby had flown in from New Orleans; Myke had flown in from Canada; and Navid all the way from Sweden. It was an honor to have brought together the disparate group of authors and clients I had worked with over the last year or two into one room, one fateful weekend in November 2015.

When it was all over, Laura and I went out to dinner with everyone that put in an application for the year-long program and a couple authors I was in some stage of publishing. The dinner after a live event is one of the most glorious feelings; it is literally like being high, the energy divine in the afterglow of meaningful accomplishment. That night on Manhattan Beach, looking out at the moonlight reflected on the vast Pacific Ocean, I smiled at just how much had happened, and how much I had changed, in less than a year since moving to Vegas.

Entrepreneurs Awakening: Ayahuasca in the Peruvian Andes

The first year on the ground in Las Vegas was wonderful in that it marked a new beginning. Ironic as it was, moving to Vegas coincided with getting serious about building a publishing business. No longer was I sitting in a student apartment in Berkeley, dreaming about the next adventure; now endless adventures lay at my doorstep. World-class musicians took up residency in Las Vegas. The best restauranteurs had flagship restaurants lining The Strip. Every week without fail, someone I knew was breezing through town. I no longer needed to travel to have a sense of liveliness, novelty, and adventure, and *that* is what I attribute to focusing my productive energies towards building a publishing company. As 2015 wound down, I had cajoled a group of my friends that were the current leadership for the Project Rockstar program to move to Vegas, and we got a house together a few miles off The Strip. Looking back on it, this was the first time I lived in a stand-alone house, and I was immediately hooked on it. We were four, sometimes five, guys in a two-story house with a pool, across the street from a park and a short drive from Las Vegas Blvd.

In 2015 I had taken Lifestyle Entrepreneurs Press from a startup in my living room to a $125,000 business. In 2016, that number would double. And in the process I went through a number of transformational experiences that rocked me to my core—both plumbing the depths of how dark I could allow my life to get, and ascending to new heights where I felt on top of the world. The first three months of the year were something of a staging ground. I was in the best shape of my adult life, eating chicken, broccoli, and noodles twice a day after going to the gym. I would sit on a couch in the living room with my laptop perched on a pillow and create the next 90-minute training for the Author to Entrepreneur Experience mastermind members I had enrolled. Then, the next day, I'd teach and train from my upstairs office with sunlight streaming in and an increasing number of books I had published adorning the wall behind me. But then a succession of events unraveled the comfortable fabric of the life I was building. Two of the mastermind members were married, each working on their own books. One of them was co-authors with another member. Somewhere around March, their marriage hit the skids, and with it the books they were working on fell by the wayside. There was acrimony and financial hardship. Then, despite having signed a year-long agreement with me, three of them dropped out. Meanwhile, another member was running into financial difficulties of his own, and before I knew it, half of the members had vanished just a few months into our journey together. I bit the bullet and wound-down the program.

For the last two years, my friend Michael Costuros, whom I had met in the first mastermind I was part of in 2013, had been inviting me to Peru on his Entrepreneurs Awakening journey. The promise was a full-life transformation in the heart of the Andes with like-minded entrepreneurs engaging in indigenous plant medicines—San Pedro and Ayahuasca. For two years, my intuition was a clear "No," and I politely declined Michael's offer. Undeterred, he asked me a third time, and as the invitation arrived, my intuition lit up like a Christmas Tree. Much to my surprise, I found myself saying yes. Michael said this year it was a men's trip. He also told me that Fast Company was sending down a film crew to make a documentary and feature article on how entrepreneurs were using Ayahuasca to have breakthroughs in their lives and businesses. The trip was scheduled for April, and we would begin meeting as a group on video calls to get acquainted and prepare for the journey weeks before liftoff. In 2016, Ayahuasca had an air of mystery to it. "The vine of death" is how Ayahuasca translates, which admittedly gives an air of foreboding to anyone who would casually approach such a powerful medicine. The death is metaphorical, however; laying to rest that which is no longer of service to birth the true authentic self from the fertilizing ashes of yesterday's life.

It is only in hindsight that I could see the subtle beauty of the process. From the moment I said "yes," things began to shift. That catalyzed the collapse of the year-long mastermind I had formed and was pushing ahead full speed with. Space was being cleared for something new to arrive, but in the moment, it just looked like a slow-motion collapse of uncharacteristically synchronistic proportions. I was also deep in the planning process for a new event I had dreamed up, a big online summit called the Book, Business & Brand Building Summit, where I would interview 20-plus authors, book marketers and industry leaders to grow my audience and prospect for new authors to publish. Also, at the same time, I had raised the price for our Done For You Publishing service package to $10,000 + 40% of book royalties and had signed a handful of clients, whom I was in various stages of the publishing process with. Charlotte, who I had first hired as an assistant, was proving very capable, and I promoted her, knowing that someone would have to take the wheel while I was offline for two weeks in Peru, imbibing the "vine of death" with 10 other male business owners deep in the Andes. When I told my housemates what I was getting ready to do, they had a thousand questions, and I didn't have the answers to any of them. But one thing was for certain, before even heading to the airport, let alone drinking from the ceremonial cup, my life was accelerating and changing in some very new ways.

The day came, and my friends dropped me off at the airport. I had been on a special diet for the last two weeks—no meat, minimal spices, no media, journaling every day, setting intentions, and slowly withdrawing from external stimulation as much as possible, turning towards inward realization. Arriving in Lima, Peru for a one-night layover, I walked through the crowded capital at night, eating only fruits and vegetables and with the impending sense of something magical about to take place. Then, the next day, a flight to Cusco. From there, a taxi ride out of the city, over the mountain, and down into the Sacred Valley of the Incas to Pisac, where I finally was deposited out front of the Paz y Luz guesthouse next to the Vilcanota River. Michael Costuros met me with a smile and gave me a strong coca candy that numbed my mouth and alleviated the headrush of arriving at 10,000 feet in elevation just hours ago. That evening all the participants of Entrepreneurs Awakening met in person for the first time, sitting in a circle on the grass underneath the towering Andes with an abundance of flowers and vegetation surrounding us. It was then I met Javier Regueiro for the first time, who insisted that he was a "plant medicine person" and not a shaman. Javier was paper thin, wearing an Adidas track suit with a shaved head smoking a mapacho cigarette with a look of qualified indifference and amusement at the group assembled before him. Right away I took a liking to him—such an unexpected figure, not an indigenous looking shaman with a ceremonial headdress but an accessible, slow-spoken maverick.

The next day, we gathered in Javier's backyard under an open-air pagoda and drank San Pedro, a Peruvian cactus that is related to peyote and known as "the heart opener" in plant medicine circles. Beginning around 8:00 a.m., we were not to speak until after the sun had set, rather to engage in our own inner experience and silent journey. What followed was a truly transcendent experience of consciousness. Yes, there were colors; kaleidoscopic visions of crystalline luminescent magnitudes. But more important was the expansion of my awareness, first into the role of observer, watching myself laying on my back in the Andes of Peru with my eyes closed. Then dissolving the concept of "I" into an infinitude of light. The moist poignant memory was hearing "I Love You, Jesse" as though someone was suddenly next to me, whispering in my ear. But then the realization dawned on me that it was me (or an aspect of infinite self), saying, "I love you"...to myself. This understanding shook me to my core. A profound feeling of self-love washed over me. The very words I had not heard with meaning for some years now pouring forth in a love letter of and for myself.

Another vision saw me standing on a precipice, facing a dragon of unfathomable proportions, blowing heavenly fire towards me with incinerating ferocity. I saw the scene from the side and noted a forcefield of light protecting me from the flames. For an eternity the dragon reared its head, spit forth white hot flames, and they wrapped around me in a luminescent egg of protective light. Then, at once, the flames ceased. The dragon lowered its head and beckoned me to climb aboard it's neck. Then, we soared through an ethereal world of colorful gaseous clouds like an endless sunrise on eternity's horizon. With one swift whip of its neck, the dragon hurled me into the air and swallowed me whole. For a moment, I felt like I lost and was now to die. Then, from inside the belly of the dragon, its skin turned translucent, its bones to crystal like diamonds. And from the safety of the stomach of a crystal dragon, we soared onward through infinity.

After what felt like a lifetime, the sun set, and Javier closed the ceremonial circle, indicating we could now speak but that it was best to remain in silence. He had prepared a delicious homemade stew, and we were allowed to eat salt for the first time in weeks to help bring our consciousness back into our bodies. That night I lay awake, looking at the expanse of stars in between the Andes with a deep sense of gratitude, awe, and wonder.

Following this induction to plant medicine, under the expert care of Javier, we rested the following day, then had our first Ayahuasca ceremony the next evening. Vastly different from the explosive, expansive, heart-opening journey with San Pedro, the "vine of death" worked its magic in a way that only those who have experienced it can relate. True to its name I simulated an experience of dying and leaving my body, through the crown chakra, spiraling up towards blinding light. I witnessed innumerable scenes of horrific violence, both being attacked and then spinning the tables, being poised to take another's life. Cycling back and forth through the duality of experiences, cycling through the wheel of karma and witnessing the suffering borne of ignorance that has plagued humanity for thousands of years. Seeing it, experiencing it, being it. Dying again, returning once more. Javier's chanting and singing percolating through the darkness. Through the glass ceiling of the Ayahuasca temple in his backyard, the Peruvian stars and dark blanket of night above contrasted with the inner visions and deep healings taking place.

Words can only do so much justice to an experience of psychedelic proportions. The bonds formed between us in that first week of ceremonies stayed strong for years to come. The second week, we journeyed up the Sacred Valley and arrived at Ollantaytambo, where 12 years prior, my sister and I had struck off to hike the Inca Trail. This time we took the scenic train to Machu Picchu and spent a magical day hiking through the ruins, sitting in circle and giving thanks for the time we had spent together as the clock wound down and a return to life began to beckon. I had let go of control in my business for the first time, empowered my team to make decisions without me, and was completely offline for close to two weeks. Much to my pleasant surprise, nothing broke. In fact, I never fully took back the reigns, and my team stepped up, relishing the new responsibilities. That, in turn, is what unlocked the next level of growth, where I stopped being involved in every single detail of each book project and started focusing on building strategic partnerships to grow my audience and come in contact with ever-more-inspiring authors.

After two weeks that felt like two years, the bonds formed on the Entrepreneurs Awakening journey were as strong as the bonds formed on eight weeks of Project Rockstar. It was the best comparable of experience I had, an immersive transformational program from which each person emerged different and new. Of the 12 total people on that trip, I went on to publish books by half of them! But most meaningful to me was the relationship that was developing with Javier Regueiro. What started in the Peruvian Andes in his backyard temples turned into a relationship with the most prolific author I've ever worked with, and it was my honor to publish *five* of his books over the coming four years. A veritable treasure trove of indigenous wisdom and plant medicine topics poured forth from Peru, and I worked diligently to document it all, resulting in *Ayahuasca*, *San Pedro / Huachuma*, *The Toe / Datura Diaries*, *A Gift of Love*, and *A Greater Gift of Love.*

But before all the books were birthed, I had a flight home to catch and a house full of eager friends who would no doubt want a full account of what had taken place. On the flight back from Lima to Las Vegas, I watched *Pawn Sacrifice*, the Bobby Fisher story, and for whatever reason, it cracked my heart wide open. I opened up a Note on my iPhone and decided to just start writing. I decided to write everything I had kept secret and hid from those closest to me. I decided to put it all down if only for me to be honest with myself. I wrote, and wrote, and *wrote*. And when I was done, my first thought was, *Well, I'm definitely not sharing that with anybody...* But then my second thought was, *What if I did... What if I shared all the parts of myself I had kept in the shadow with everyone I had ever met and trusted sunlight to be the best disinfectant, absolving me of the weight of the words I had kept bottled up inside?* By the time I landed, I had convinced myself to do just that.

So, I present to you here much of what I wrote on that fateful flight home.

Words From My Heart, Born in the Peruvian Andes

Now I am returned from a 10-day retreat in Peru where I partook in a number of plant-medicine ceremonies under expert guidance and care.

Not to get "high" but because Ayahuasca is the one thing I've ever read about that has the potential to give perspective on a situation like mine.

It worked.

Now I understand myself on a level of depth I almost can't believe is real.

But it is as real as the words I'm writing and you are reading now.

This understanding is not a function of some powerful entheogenic substance showing me "God," or really anything external whatsoever.

This understanding is one born from something so simple yet so profound: Surrender and forgiveness.

Surrendering the illusions and identities I have held in exchange for self-acceptance; self-love.

And forgiveness. Not forgiveness of anyone I may have ever perceived harmed me, did me wrong in any way, but forgiving myself.

Forgiving myself for all the times I trespassed my own values for expediency or out of habit.

Forgiving myself for the needless pain and suffering I have inflicted on myself.

Forgiving myself for all the emotional attachment and artifice I have carried for the people who I perceive myself as having harmed, inadvertently or intentionally.

At the end of it all, these words give me both solace and strength:

"I release, I surrender, I am willing. I love you, Jesse"

I release myself from all of the unnecessary constructs and constraints my hyperactive intellect has created and perpetuated over the years.

"I surrender." All of the arguments, entrepreneurial decisions, learning of languages, and everything I have done to prove my worth to myself or anyone else. I surrender, therefore anyone who would face me in a spirit of competition—wins.

"I am willing." I am willing to engage with anyone, any situation, any opportunity to learn and grow with a spirit of willingness that does not seek to predetermine or influence the outcome, but rather to serve as an opportunity to learn and experience all that this life has to offer.

"I love you, Jesse." Because so much of what I have done in life has, at some level, been to seek validation, I didn't realize that the love and validation I have sought externally has always lived in my own heart.

"I release, I surrender, I am willing."

Very willing.

Willing enough to lay myself bare and not be concerned with whatever consequences that may entail.

Willing enough to love myself, and through that love be capable of truly loving someone else, and all people.

For it is true in this world that for something to grow, something else must die.

I could put it more softly, but why bother?

So I am willing to let myself die in order to grow.

Like a snake that outgrows its skin and leaves it behind in order to grow to its full potential.

I am willing to leave all that I've done and the person I have been behind, that I may grow to realize my full potential.

By conventional measure, I would make a terrible politician, for I do not seek power.

Only power over myself.

And power is different than force.

Power radiates from within, while force acts from without.

Gravity is a force. Love is a power.

Force seeks subjugation and submission.

Power seeks to empower, and thereby become more empowered.

So I share this in a spirit of willingness and love, if only for my own sake, but also with the hope that it may empower others. Empower you. And thereby further empower me. And so on in a virtuous cycle.

Through these ceremonies with Ayahuasca I have felt first-hand what it is to die, and death does not end it, but simply marks the beginning of what comes next.

I won't say that I am not scared of death. But I will die, and so will everyone on Earth alive as I write this. In light of that morbid reminder, I am most willing to live.

To truly live. To live without fear, and with great joy.

Because life is beautiful, and worth experiencing in its totality.

"Therefore, I release, I surrender, I am willing. I love you, Jesse."

And because of that, I am capable to love you!

So, I love you.

Thank you for reading and may you be empowered to live with a spirit of love and willingness for all of your days.

:)

Transformational Experiences Catalyze Novelty

Well what do you think? Were you moved by my account of journeying to Peru and engaging in plant medicines? What did you think of the resulting writing? Yes, I know you're reading a book—we aren't having a two-way conversation at the moment. But, you actually can write me and let me know what you think—now or anytime: Jesse@JesseKrieger.com. Best of all, I'll reply!

Now that we got that out of the way, let's jump back into the storyline. This is where things really start to get interesting...

I'm aware of the fact that each chapter of writing this chronology of my life experiences brings me closer to the present. The closer I get, the more alive, recent, and fresh the emotional experiences that accompany these stories get. It's one thing to write with perspective and objectivity about what I was doing 20 years ago living in Europe, 15 years ago in a rock band, even 10 years ago just graduating Cal and with my first book just published. But now, spiraling in towards present time, some of these storylines are still alive and unfolding. Moreover, there are fresh emotions and current relationships involved in some of what comes next. So, with that said, I'm going to give it my best to do these remaining chapters justice, leading up to the climactic cataclysm that immediately preceded sitting down to write this book. Here we go...

Back in Las Vegas after a transformational two weeks in Peru. For all the visceral experiences of consciousness that unfolded in the Andes, and for all the amazing bonds of brotherhood formed on that trip, the real work begins, entering back into life with a new perspective. I conveyed my experiences as best I could to my friends I lived with. Many of them were moved and went on to sit in ceremony with Ayahuasca themselves, having their own profound experiences that catalyzed all sorts of interesting changes in their lives. For me, the real impact of that transformational journey unfolded over the rest of 2016, and in a number of ways extends up to present time as I'm writing these words in 2022.

With book publishing, I picked up where I left off. The year-long mastermind of authors I was running had unwound, but I was also signing new authors every one to two weeks. I also kicked into high gear, preparing to run the Book, Business & Brand Building Summit where I had 10 days of live interviews lined up, as well as 30-plus promotional partners committed to event. I was eating healthy, exercising almost every day, and felt a renewed fire in my belly to build and achieve. The summer was on the horizon, and Las Vegas weather was marching back to the triple digits. The crew of guys I lived with were making plans to hit EDC (Electric Daisy Carnival), the biggest rave in the world that takes place each summer on the Las Vegas Speedway. A close friend of mine connected me with a girl he was dating named Cassie to have her come to the festival with us, as he was overseas. I had met her briefly some months back and didn't think much of it, so I messaged her and we chit chatted, then decided to meet up for drinks to talk about festival logistics.

Since Angelina and I had broken up, I went back to what was familiar; dating a handful of girls at a time, none too seriously. Honestly, at this stage of life, I considered myself polyamorous. Years of being a dating coach, traveling the world, and meeting girls in nightclubs had made it seem natural to take a casual approach to sex and dating. I knew the friend that connected me with Cassie was dating other people and, at the time, Cassie just so happened to be a stripper at Spearmint Rhino, the top strip club in America. What totally took me by surprise, however, was when we met up for drinks at the Chandelier Bar in The Cosmopolitan, immediately sparks started flying. I mean, the chemistry was electric! Laughing, joking, having a riot of a time, we drank and laughed and talked and laughed some more. Then I invited her back to my place, dangling the possibility of singing to her in Chinese and a few more drinks as incentive. So we hit pause on the good times, both drove over to my place, then picked it back up with a passion. I followed through on singing in Chinese, and we both had another couple drinks. In fact, the passion became so vividly electric that we started making out and then had sex for hours upon hours upon hours. This was like soul-shattering sex, like every adolescent fantasy spilling over to the present moment and replaying 100 times until literally the sun came up and finally, finally ended collapsed in a heap, sleeping for a few hours intertwined in each other's arms.

We woke up around noon. She instantly became worried, actually borderline freaking out that she had just violated the trust of our friend that connected us. I came to and became pretty concerned myself, both for the reason she was upset and for her current state of mind. *Oh, no. Did I just screw up Big Time?* I messaged my friend and told him what happened. While he wasn't thrilled, it also probably wasn't the most surprising thing either. In that first hour of regaining consciousness, it seemed that everything was fine and we just had ourselves one hell of a night. As she left, and I eventually came downstairs to my housemates staring in disbelief (since they heard everything that transpired for the last, oh, 10 hours), it felt like a little bit of a *Twilight Zone* moment. But then we all kind of shrugged and went on with our day. Over the years, we've all had no shortage of wild nights, but this one just hit a little close to home. I knew I had crossed a line even if it was blurry or hard to define. Over the coming days leading up to EDC, we saw each other a few more times. Each time it was insane sexual chemistry, and then we were at the biggest rave in the world having the most epic party imaginable, and shortly thereafter we became inseparable. On the one hand, wow, what an amazing feeling to have a mind-blowing connection on just about every level with someone whose life was so vastly different than mine. On the other hand, I was becoming more aware of how I had violated my friendship with the guy who connected us to make plans for EDC.

So, the Summer of 2016 was a time that took years to put into perspective. Here I was, falling in love with a stripper, who was dating my friend, and on the surface level, that was all fine, but at a deeper level, a real dark shadow aspect of my personality was making itself known in the most vexing of ways. Cassie and I had formed a connection that was undeniable, and in the best of times, anyone who saw us together gushed at the magic between us. But at the same time, I was revolted with myself for what I was allowing to happen. I had violated a brotherly code of conduct with a good friend, but I felt like I was strapped into a rollercoaster ride where I couldn't eject, but also had no idea where the ride was going to end. Project Rockstar rolled around, we all moved out of our house and into a set of suites in The Cosmopolitan. The program had evolved from its humble but powerful roots in Brick Lane, London in 2008 to now encompass numerous wraparound suites at the top hotel in Vegas, a six-figure budget for bottle service and partying at clubs, and a world-class roster of instructors and guest lecturers pouring into the current class of Rockstars.

It's wild; over six years later, I still see it all so clearly. Dating a stripper, teaching entrepreneurship, publishing books, making increasingly more money. But underneath it all, there was a fatalism. The casual dating that felt fine for years and years now had a sharp edge to it. I realized I had damaged my friendship beyond repair with the guy who connected us, by virtue of continuing to see her and both of us having increasing feelings. What I didn't know how to do then was change.

In the midst of building Lifestyle Entrepreneurs Press I would regularly deliver live trainings to partner audiences. I had a presentation called Publishing Masterclass where I would teach all about self-publishing, traditional publishing, and then what we did, which was hybrid publishing. I'd answer everyone's questions on the line, give the best advice I could, then invite people to book a publishing consultation with me if they were interested in exploring publishing with us. On September 20, 2016, I delivered a Publishing Masterclass to a partner's audience named John Eggen. Two people scheduled a publishing consultation with me as a result. One of them was a man named Dale Halaway.

One week later, I had a call with Dale Halaway, and it was like time stood still. I vividly remember exactly where I was. My friend Akira was having a party at his condo in Santa Monica. I went into the guest bedroom to take the call. And I can see the look on my face now as I answered the phone and Dale introduced himself. Interestingly enough, he shared with me that he felt a deep recognition at the sound of my voice. He had heard me on the presentation, but this was the first we had spoken directly. Dale Halaway, as it turns out, has led *thousands* of seminars across a 40-year career as a teacher, speaker, consultant, and transformational leader. He shared this with me and he shared his vision to create a trilogy of books, what we now call The Transformation Trilogy. It sounded like a beautiful project, and I said I'd love to be involved.

I was in the midst of planning Bestseller Summit Live 2016, this time to be a three-day live event at the Sheraton near LAX. Dale and I had signed a publishing agreement, and I invited him as my guest to the event, which he graciously accepted. Cassie accompanied me to LA, always amused at my explosive entrepreneurial drive, and she attended the event, too, which made me feel like superman on stage. This year we had nearly 60 attendees, and I created a VIP level where all meals where included and Laura Gisborne and I would do a deep dive on the evening of Day 2 with all the VIPs. The event was a peak experience in my thirties. Even at the early stages of building a publishing company, I had amassed an audience of thousands and had published over a dozen books. My dad, bless his heart, has attended every live event I've ever run and he was in the audience smiling up at me. There, as well, was Dale Halaway, whom I was just at the beginning stages of a publishing partnership with. There were dozens of authors and attendees, and I espoused everything I knew about writing, publishing, and promoting a book.

Dale Halaway has gone on to become a dear friend and trusted mentor. We recently released the second book in his trilogy, *Transform Your Destiny*. But back in 2016, he came into my life in divine timing to help shine a light for me to understand myself at increasingly deeper levels. His presence in my life set into sharp contrast how I was living and the choices I was making with Cassie. And although I was always on when it came to calls with authors, speaking on stage, or recording interviews, Dale illuminated the darker side of my nature, which was drinking too much, living too loose, and ultimately leaking my life force energy with the lower-energy decisions I was making in parallel to a business that was doubling in size from the year before.

The deeper significance of all this is that Dale Halaway remains the only author I've had the honor of publishing, where I became *his* student. The transformational seminars that Dale leads are the most powerful, riveting, and life-altering I've ever come across. And I've been in the business of identifying powerful leaders and supporting them through the writing, publishing, and book promotion process for years.

After my time in Peru, my life was in overdrive. I was also coming face-to-face with some of my shadow aspects. I had destroyed a friendship in the process of falling for a girl, and we were both seeing other people in the process (talk about confusing). What cracked open in Peru directly led to what became a destructive relationship, which devastated me when it ended a few months later, but it also sent up a cosmic flare of sorts that attracted Dale into my life at this important juncture.

Moving towards the end of 2016, I reached out to David Hancock, the CEO of Morgan James Publishing and *my* publisher for *Lifestyle Entrepreneur* and asked him for an introduction to Ingram Publisher Services. I had decided that it was time to build a "real" publishing company, one that had a distribution partner that could reach into every retailer in America, as well as the UK, Europe, and Australia. David graciously made the introduction. But Ingram said we weren't at the size they needed yet; they said we needed to sell over $250,000 worth of books per year to really consider us. They made a connection to a smaller distributor and suggested we start there and they'd follow the story, then when the time was right, we could revisit it. Thus were the seeds of the future planted and watered in the most wondrous of ways in the most wild and fast-paced time of my thirties. Well, at least, the wildest and most fast-paced time so far...

Getting Books in Stores and On Shelves

Towards the end of 2016, I accepted an invitation to join Summit at Sea, a cruise ship full of creatives, entrepreneurs and business leaders setting sail into international waters for four days of curated conversations and connection. The ship set sail in Miami and the date of departure was the day after the US presidential election. Like many people, I stayed up late to see who our next president would be, and it wasn't until around 2:00 a.m. Eastern Time that the election was called and Donald Trump was to be our next president. Just a few hours later, at the Port of Miami, there was plenty of conversation about this very topic, as we were about to sail away and have no internet connection or cell service for the next four days. *What a wild time to be alive*, I thought as I walked up the gangplank and onto the ship, switching off my phone and settling in for the journey. On that trip I got to chat with the creator of MTV, sat front row for a fireside chat with the CEO of Google, and met the founder of Four Sigmatic as well as many other interesting entrepreneurs. One of them was Nicole Yershon, daughter of a UK advertising legend, sitting in a hot tub with a cowgirl hat on hundreds of miles from land. We ended up signing a publishing deal, and a couple months later, I flew to London to work with her for four days of interviews, creating content for her book *Rough Diamond: Turning Disruption Into Advantage in Business and Life.*

When I was in London, I met a long-time friend Mark van Stratum, with whom I was working with to publish his book, *Drug of Choice: The Inspiring True Story of the One-Armed Criminal Who Mastered Love and Made Millions.* In between author interviews at SoHo House and dinners near Piccadilly Circus, I was loving the way my life was unfolding. I had made the transition from traveling the world for fun and fancy, to getting flown around the globe to teach dating bootcamps, and I was traveling the world yet again, but to help interesting authors create and publish their books. The way I had the publishing company set up in early 2017, we were using an array of different online platforms to publish books and make them available in all formats; digital, paperback, hardcover, and audiobook. The introduction David Hancock made to Ingram resulted in them connecting me with an independent book distributor called Midpoint Trade. Top of my list was to get a deal signed with them so we could get our books in stores, libraries, and eventually airport bookstores as well. We had been negotiating for a couple months, and by the end of Quarter 1, 2017, we signed the contract.

This was a key development as far as I was concerned, as it meant we now had a team of book sales reps meeting with book buyers at chains like Barnes & Noble, Target, Indigo Chapters, and more. I had been charging $10,000 and 40% of book royalties for our Done For You Publishing package, and had signed over 10 authors in 2016, but felt like I was topping out at what I could charge without in-store book distribution. With the Midpoint deal signed, I raised our prices to $15,000 and 50% of Net Royalties, which we calculated as gross sales minus returns, print costs, and any distribution fees. Relative to other publishing companies, it was fair and also a unique model, as we did full-service book production work on the front end. We had an editorial team, a design team, a layout and formatting specialist, an audio engineer for audiobook production, and a few back-office staff, plus Charlotte, who was going into her third year working for me and had become my right-hand operations manager.

I saw the future growing brighter as we got to work preparing all our books to go into Midpoint's distribution system and started learning the ropes for all that entailed. The virtual summit I ran last year, the Book, Business & Brand Building Summit, had done fairly well and added around 6,000 people to my audience, all of whom had watched me interview 20-plus bestselling authors and book marketing experts across a marathon 10 days of live broadcasts. I was so wiped out by the end of that I was about to collapse, but I had figured out the virtual summit model and knew I could do it bigger and better this year in a different way. So, with our distribution deal signed, our prices raised, and our value proposition as strong as it had ever been, I decided to run a big online summit and call it Bestseller Summit Online. For the last two years, I had run Bestseller Summit LIVE as a two- and then three-day event in Los Angeles, so it made sense to leverage that brand name for an online summit a few months before the live event. This time I would interview over 25 authors, publishers, and book marketers, some of whom were *New York Times* bestsellers and ran multi-million-dollar businesses, but I decided to make it five days and have all the interviews pre-recorded, then do live on-air panel discussions. Much more manageable than 10 days of live interviews every day!

The way I saw 2017 unfolding was to run Bestseller Summit Online in May, then spend the next couple months signing new authors that I met through that big promotion. Then we would go live with Midpoint and have our books distributed by summer, so I booked a booth at BookExpo NYC and invited our authors to come out and do in-booth signings in June. July would be a little break in the action with Project Rockstar once again rolling through Las Vegas and a chance to catch up with my international crew of friends that would be in town. Then, in August we would start publishing our Fall season with in-store distribution. We had 15 books lined up to publish in 2017, and my team was working like a well-oiled machine. Then, in October, I would host Bestseller Summit LIVE once more in LA and invite all the authors we published that year to come and grace the stage. If that all sounds like a lot of work, well, it definitely was. But, at the same time, I was loving working with so many interesting authors and learning a ton from each project, while making more and more money in the process.

The summit preparations were pretty extensive, and I was interviewing two to three people a week, plus I had hired a partner manager named Tom who helped coordinate over 50 people with audiences of their own to promote the summit. To incentivize people to promote, I offered 50 percent of the revenue from selling the recordings of the summit. This year I stacked a ton of bonuses, including a ticket to Bestseller Summit LIVE and a complete author website template that my team designed, which looked better than most websites I had seen from self-published authors. When the summit promotions started, it was magic. We got over 8,500 people registered; thousands and thousands of new people joining my audience. The engagement on the summit was great, and because I did all the interviews in advance, I could actually enjoy the experience instead of being nose to the grindstone, doing all the interviews live. All in all it cost about $30,000 to put on Bestseller Summit Online and it made a small net profit, but the big impact was thousands of new authors joining my audience and massive exposure from interviewing a who's-who of book publishing in the process.

Shortly after the Summit wrapped up, I had a flood of new interest in book publishing, which was the goal, and I was on 7 to 10 phone and Zoom calls most days. The focus shifted to prepping for BookExpo NYC, and a handful of authors had committed to coming out. We set up a booth right smack dab in the middle of the Javits Center, and for the first time, I saw the entire book publishing industry in one place. Ingram, the largest book distributor in the world, had a massive presence at BookExpo, and I made sure to go over and make the rounds with their execs and team members, inviting them to our booth where we had back-to-back authors signing books and a display of all the books we published available for visitors to browse. BookExpo was a major rush. The first day was one of the best days of my life—I must have met 100 people, from foreign rights buyers, to bookstore owners, to librarians, to book marketers and beyond. By the time Day 1 was over, my feet were positively aching and my voice was just about shot. But I toughened up, pounded a coffee, and went out to have dinner with authors and network with even more people on the sidelines of the event. When it was all over, I walked back to The W in Times Square, marveling at how my life has evolved over the years and how now, of all things, I was a book publisher with a distribution deal, a view of the New York skyline, and some very sore feet.

Just a few weeks later, our first books would begin to come out in stores, and two of the first were Javier Regueiro's *Ayahuasca: Soul Medicine of the Amazon Jungle* and *San Pedro / Huachuma: Opening the Pathways of the Heart.* I had been diligently working with him since last year in Peru and had developed a close relationship with this truly powerful plant medicine maestro, who was one of the most interesting people I've ever met. That made it all the more painful when we ran into printing issues going into the release of his books, the first of our fall publishing season. I was on a family vacation in Seward, Alaska, when I got the news and I flipped—just flew off the rails. I called Midpoint numerous times, yelling at them to get it right and get this fixed. It felt like banging my head against a brick wall, and I realized for the first time that the reality of working with a distributor is I didn't have all the levers of control in my hands. Finally, after days of panic that spilled over to our otherwise serene vacation in rural Alaska, we got it sorted and, thank goodness, the releases ended up taking place without further incident. At long last, I could now say Lifestyle Entrepreneurs Press books are available wherever books are sold and it was true. Every bookstore and library now had access to our catalog, and we published a book nearly every week in August and September of 2017.

As we moved into October, I got all ready to run Bestseller Summit LIVE for the third consecutive year. Thinking back to how nervous I was in 2015, I smiled. This time we had everything dialed in. Laura Gisborne graciously agreed to be my co-host once more, I had a snazzy blue suit and pocket square fitted, and around 10 authors I had published showed up, many of them getting stage time and all of them getting pictures and videos to use for their own promotions. My dad came through for the third time, and since he has been working on his own books since I was a teenager, I invited him on stage and gave him the mic to share whatever he wanted. Even if his books hadn't come out yet, I wanted to honor him with the experience that I gave our published authors, and he, in turn, used most of his time to tell the audience what an amazing son he had and how proud he was. I stood in the back of the room, head ascended in silent salute, mic'ed up with a lavaliere microphone in a three-piece suit, with a tear in my eye, taking in the immensity of the beautiful father-son moment.

This ended up being the last year I ran the event. Not because it wasn't fun, cause it most certainly was, but it cost a lot of money and was a huge time investment, and at the end of the day, I didn't really sign new authors as a result of it. It was more of a showcase for the authors and books we published, combined with teaching and training, plus a bunch of meals together as a group. I was quickly learning that having a book distribution partner and getting in stores was an expensive proposition. One of the books we published, *The Concussion Repair Manual* by Dr. Dan Engle (who I had also met in Peru), brought this lesson home in an unexpectedly wonderful way. One day, I opened my email and saw Tim Ferriss, the *New York Times* bestselling author of *The 4-Hour Workweek* had sent out an email to his one-million-plus readers. The first line in it was "What I'm reading: *The Concussion Repair Manual...*" with a link to the book on Amazon. *Holy cow! This is amazing!* I thought. Then I clicked through and saw we had just about sold out all of our inventory within hours of the email going out. Well, that meant firing up the printing presses and spending close to $10,000 to print more books as fast as possible to keep up with the demand.

As 2017 came to a close, and I looked over our profit and loss statement, I was pleased to see we had nearly doubled in size to over $400,000 in gross revenue. A year of hard work, diligence, and experimentation had grown our audience over 10,000 people, placed our books in stores, and I was starting to build a name for myself and the press. At the same time, I was taking on more debt and expanding lines of credit to accommodate the growth. My team had grown in size, it was expensive printing thousands of books, and running the business was becoming more costly all around. But I took it all in stride and had my sights set on making 2018 our biggest year yet.

Signing With the Biggest Book Distributor on Earth

The amazing thing about running all my work meetings through a calendar synced across all my devices is I can look back and see exactly what I was doing years into the past. 2018 started off rich with potential; in January alone I had close to 100 scheduled meetings, and that essentially set the pace for the year, which means I probably had around 1,000 meetings, interviews, team calls, and mentorship sessions in 2018 alone. My approach has always been to move all the balls into someone else's court while on a call, which can mean sending an email, making an introduction, or instructing my team to do something. So that means thousands of actions being taken for the sake of growing Lifestyle Entrepreneurs Press over the course of the year. All this activity to keep up with the demands of growing a publishing business, building my audience, appearing on media and podcast interviews, and working with mentors to help guide my way. The year was explosive, but it also preceded a very painful reckoning that was just over the horizon.

Since moving to Las Vegas in 2015 I had realized the vision I had that moving here would be the catalyst to really build my publishing company. That had now resulted in over three years of running live events in LA, hosting two large online summits that added close to 15,000 people to my audience, exhibiting at BookExpo in NYC, and signing an in-store distribution deal to expand the reach of our books. Day to day, I thoroughly enjoyed most calls with our authors. Each publishing project is an opportunity to deep dive into a new topic, and of particular interest to me was getting to know the author personally and witnessing the process of creation that culminates in a book. In just about every case there is a moment where it "becomes real" for them and the energy shifts. Whether that is writing the final chapter to their book, or receiving the first print copy (like it was for me), or announcing the release date to everyone they know, there are plenty of milestones on the road to Launch Day. I was becoming adept at helping now dozens of authors navigate the winding road to releasing their book.

I was also starting to get pretty good at the front-end conversation, the publishing consultation, where I would meet with an author for the first time and learn about their vision. On those calls I was refining a process that was becoming very effective. First, I'd say something along the lines of "Well, I've read through everything you sent me and I have a sense for the book you're working on, but I'd love to hear you share your vision with me and hear what you'd like to see happen with your book." Then, I'd sit back and listen. Deep listening. My full attention on not just their words but their tone of voice, their confidence, how they presented themselves and their idea. That would go for 5 to 10 minutes, and then I would speak again. This time I could reflect back to them what I heard, bring their attention to the potential for their book as I understood it, and then talk them through the process from exactly where they were at to having a published—and ideally *bestselling*—book. If we both felt it was a good fit, then I'd share the pricing for our Done For You Publishing package, which at this time was $15,000 and 50 percent net royalties if they had a manuscript in development or up to $25,000 if I was going to help them create the book as part of the process. I estimate that out of every three to four publishing consultations I had, we would wind up signing an author and generating revenue for the business.

My team was now getting close to 10 people, with Charlotte becoming chief operating officer and two other managers working alongside her. Then about six others working on editing, design, layout, and marketing. Our payroll was pushing $20,000/month, and we were bringing in around $40,000/mo. Quite an expensive business; at least the way I was running it, where we gave extensive attention and support to each author for many months before their book came out. Printing costs were going up, as we were selling more books and our distribution deal required us to print books and have them in the warehouse before we could accept sales. So even though I was signing deals and we were selling books and bringing in tens of thousands in revenue every month, I was still adding to credit card debt, taking our lines of credit and focusing a decent amount of energy on the financial needs of the business. I told myself it was all worth it if we could get close to $250,000 in book sales and sign a deal with Ingram, my number-one goal for business development. Ingram is the cornerstone of the book publishing industry in many ways, with integrated printing and warehousing divisions, a team of over 50 book sales reps, and practically every bookstore in the world has an account with them, as they account for around 30 percent of all books sold.

As we moved towards the summer months, we got another booth at BookExpo NYC, this time in a prime location. I sent out word to our authors, and around seven of them committed to coming to do book signings. I was in touch with Ingram leading up to BookExpo, and they suggested we meet at the event to revisit the idea of taking us on. Once again, the first day of BookExpo was one of the best days of my life. We had six hours of book signings scheduled in our booth and a little library set-up with comfortable chairs for attendees to relax and peruse our catalog. Before the doors opened, I huddled up with our authors and we said a prayer. I told them my plan to bring the vice president of acquisitions for Ingram over to our booth, and that when I did to lay it on thick. A few hours into the opening day, with a crowd of people around our booth to get free books and meet the authors, I went over and invited the VP to swing by. He came over, and I gave the signal. Author after author approached him as he walked up, offering a signed copy of their book and saying how much we supported them as a publisher. Then he was in our booth and we sat and chatted for a moment. I told him "Good news! We're on track to hit $250,000 in book sales this year, and I know we could continue to grow with you as our distribution partner."

He took it all in, congratulated me on the hard work, and said, "This looks very promising. Let's set up a time to chat after Book-Expo. I think we can put a deal on the table for you." My heart skipped a beat, but I played it cool. Well, at least, until he walked out of the booth and turned the corner. Then I dropped to my knees in the middle of the expo floor, raised my arms to the sky, and thanked the publishing gods!

His word was good, and a few weeks later, I received a distribution and sales agreement from the largest book distributor in the world. *Wow*, I thought, *the hard work and long days are paying off.* We went back and forth over the next few weeks, and I asked for a couple concessions. Not that I had a ton of negotiating leverage, but I wanted them to know I was paying attention and taking the relationship seriously. Then we got it done. The contract was complete and ready for signatures. and I received an invitation to their global headquarters in La Vergne, Tennessee, just south of Nashville, my former home. By the time October rolled around, I was touching down in Nashville and it was like two worlds colliding. I saw my former band mate and first business partner, Jake Harsh, who still lived in Nashville. We caught up and reminisced, amazed that it had been 13 years since we lived on Music Row. Then, the next day, I drove down to Ingram headquarters for a publisher on-boarding seminar to meet the team, learn their processes, and get access to all the systems we would be using. Ingram's headquarters are massive, and I got to tour their printing facility, with million-dollar printers spinning out books like lightning, and their main warehouse, which houses over 19 million books at any given time. Consider that the UC Berkeley library, which is four stories and stretches nearly a quarter mile underground has around three million books, and you get an idea for the size and scale of the operation. All in all, it felt like "coming home." I had worked and waited for this very moment for years and now I was here, getting to know the team, having dinner with the execs, and dreaming bigger than ever.

That night, after a long day of meetings and seminars, I had booked myself in the Opryland Hotel. The Opryland is a city unto itself with a massive glass structure containing a forest, river, myriad walkways, a dozen restaurants, and countless stores and scenic vistas. In my room, looking out over an expanse of trees, I talked to my team and gave them the news. "You did it," Charlotte said proudly.

"*We* did it," I said in return. "Now let's sell some books!"

The rest of the year was spent transitioning over nearly 50 books into Ingram's system and learning the complex process of setting up new titles for release. My team was working over-time. I was pushing myself to the hilt and preparing to present our Spring 2019 releases to the whole Ingram Sales Team the first week of December. It was a mad rush, and we got it all done. Come December I walked into their West Coast offices, in Berkeley, California, of all places, to present our forthcoming titles to dozens of seasoned sales reps. My life had come full circle in more ways than one, from having a new business partnership that would bring me to Nashville a couple times a year, and now back in Berkeley nearly five years after moving to Vegas; our deal with Ingram gave me myriad ways to reflect on the places I've called home and what my life was like then versus now. I was nervous as could be going into the sales presentation but was also over-prepared and after the first few moments, with my cheeks flushed staring out across the boardroom, I found my footing and previewed our forthcoming books with all the passion and gusto I could summon. The team gave me a round of applause when I was done, and I snapped a picture for posterity, then we all had a dinner mixer on Shattuck Avenue. What a trip, from a student studying in coffee shops here close to a decade prior, then living right up the street where I started the publishing company in my living room, to dining with the executive team of the biggest and best book distributor in the game. It's moments like these that I savor the rich tapestry of life spread out over the table of time.

From Commanding Highs to Crushing Lows

My birthday is December 19, and on my birthday in 2018, we had a team call to celebrate our best year yet. Not only had we signed the deal with Ingram; we had broken $500,000 in revenue for the first time and had a slate of exciting books lined up for 2019. I remember looking at the faces of my team, smiling as they wished me happy birthday and expressing my gratitude for how we all pulled together to make some publishing magic happen this year. What I couldn't see at the time was a storm of discontent brewing under the surface. In my mind I had empowered my team, paid them fairly, and often times didn't even take a salary myself. We had a few authors that caused problems from time to time, but I effectively glossed over that and delegated it to Charlotte to find an equitable solution. Looking back now, I would say I was doing something of an emotional bypass, focusing on the areas of the business I enjoyed; being the face of the company and signing new authors while managing our key relationships. Charlotte knew me well, and I gave her wide operating latitude to get what I needed done with minimal spillover to my schedule. She had all my credit cards, all our passwords, and could even impersonate me well on calls with companies if I asked her to so I didn't have to deal with the details.

Going into 2019, I was focused on the momentum we were building and the books we were getting ready to publish. But there was a storm on the horizon, and it was about to knock me down for the count. Credit card bills were mounting, and I was refinancing high-interest loans for to smooth out cash flow that was up and down. But I always made payroll, and we paid author royalties every quarter without question. I was all-in and had personally guaranteed all the financing for the company. Plus, it was my signature on every publishing deal next to the authors, so even though we were structured as a corporation, I was responsible for everything that happened in the company, even if I tried to brush our problems under the table. Well, leading up our spring publishing season, one of those problems burst out into the open and kickstarted a cascade of pain. An author who had paid close to $25,000, and who we had been working with for over a year, finally yielding a manuscript ready to publish, threatened to sure me and demanded a full refund. What really got me was the author had a sleazy lawyer write a threatening letter making all sorts of wild accusations. I told my team, who had long since identified him as a "problem author," and they were shocked but also not totally surprised. I asked my dad for advice, and he said effectively that the best defense is a good offense and if he was threatening to sue me, I should take the initiative and file a lawsuit against him first.

I filed a suit against the author for fraud and breach of contract since we had already promoted the book as one of our main titles for spring. No shorter than two weeks later, I was informed by Charlotte that she was quitting and starting her own business. What kind of business? A publishing services company. Well, imagine that. My remaining team was shell-shocked. Or at least that's how they played it. "What are we going to do without her?" they asked. She was in charge of delegating work and overseeing most of the company operations at the time. I said we will keep moving forward and adapt. But then one week later, another of my main managers left. Then the following week my third and final lieutenant resigned. Turns out they had all been working together behind the scenes for who knows how long, laying the groundwork to launch their own business, and now it all spilled out into the open. From celebrating our biggest deal and best year yet just a few weeks prior, now my whole management team had resigned and I was in a lawsuit with who was supposed to be our biggest spring author. I was crushed. Flattened. Just devastated.

Over the past couple years, Dale Halaway and I had grown closer, and he became a mentor of mine just as I had become a student of his, attending his transformational seminars. For the first year or so of going to his classes, I always found myself making some excuse for why I couldn't stay for the whole course. Every reason was convincing, but all of them were coming from the same unhealed place that had manifested this painful exodus of my team. The unhealed shadow aspects of myself were making themselves known in an unmistakable way, and it was not comfortable, to say the least. But, over the last year, I had been courting Dale to be an advisor and mentor to our authors as well as myself. While the storm was brewing, the first cracks of lightning struck, Dale and I had reached an agreement for him to join the company. I told him everything that was going on, and he gave me compassionate support. The exact same timeframe that my team left is when he agreed to come on board. In hindsight it was divinely orchestrated.

In the moment, I was glad to have a trusted mentor, author, and friend advising me when it felt like everything I worked so hard for was collapsing right in front of me.

Over the following weeks and months, I essentially re-learned how to run the company I had started. I had taken my hands off the proverbial wheel and was paying staff tens of thousands of dollars each month to handle everything I didn't want to do. It was quite an adjustment, but I recommitted to myself and our authors, who were asking why all the people they had dealt with were no longer with the company. For months I navigated the transition, had countless uncomfortable conversations, humbled myself, and kept recommitting to do whatever needed to be done. Finally, I got a handle on the situation and the tides started to turn just a little. Turns out filing the lawsuit gave me an advantage. The author who threatened me never actually filed a suit, and I was able to settle with a guarantee that the author was barred from disparaging me moving forward. What I also found out was with a little ingenuity and focus, I was able to streamline the work that a full-time three-person management team was doing all by myself.

2019 was a year of transition and a painful coming to grips with the full reality of what I was building. By the middle of the year, after months of hustle, negotiation, humility, and more hustle, there was a semblance of normalcy on the horizon. Coming into the year I was so looking forward to celebrating our first publishing season integrated with Ingram with my team. As it turned out, I managed to get through the launches of numerous books practically without a team. It was the first time in close to five years that revenue declined. From having our best year ever in 2018, revenues dropped around 35 percent in 2019, much of it from regrouping in the first half of the year.

But once I had a handle on the operations and was back in the driver's seat with my hands on the controls, I refocused and started to dream again. Regardless of everything that happened, I landed on my feet. Now I had Dale in my corner, advising me personally and on the company operations, and we were starting to think about the second book in his trilogy, *Transform Your Destiny*. I began to explore new partnerships and collaborations and was starting to generate new interest from authors who wanted to publish with us.

One of the opportunities that came online towards the end of the year was from a friend of mine, Guy Vincent, who was the CEO of Publishizer. He had started a crowdfunding platform for authors where authors could pre-sell their book and raise funds that could be used to self-publish or to attract a publisher like Lifestyle Entrepreneurs Press. We had used Publishizer a few times to help launch books we were publishing, and I had spent time with Guy and his team at BookExpo over the last couple years. Turns out, he wanted to sell the company and move on to try something new. We talked a number of times about how this could work, and I was interested, as I saw it as a way to have an endless stream of new potential authors to publish. Best case scenario, I saw it as a way for authors to prove their book concept and marketing chops by raising money, then I would sign them to take their book across the finish line and into our distribution channels.

We were getting closer to a deal structure, but then hit a snag. He had a few investors, and they didn't want to sell on the terms Guy and I were discussing. But they were open to finding a deal structure where they could still be involved and not get bought out. Guy came to Las Vegas, and we had a dinner and long conversation, finally arriving at what we both believed would be a win for everyone. I would take over operations of Publishizer and operate the platform. Instead of buying the company, we would pay a monthly licensing fee and keep the rest of the team working on bringing authors to the platform. The crowdfunding revenue would become revenue for Lifestyle Entrepreneurs Press, and we would still pay out authors who wanted to take their share of the proceeds and publish elsewhere. But we would also have an inside track to try and sign publishing deals with promising authors before other publishers were in touch with them. The investors and his team all agreed. We had a deal!

After a year of trials and tribulations, we still made around $350,000 in revenue and had a big slate of authors ready to publish in 2020. We were scheduled to go live with Publishizer in January 2020, and I had a few other partnerships lined up that were referring authors and books to us. Things were starting to look good again, and I'm glad I didn't give up when the going got tough.

2020 – A Year for the Books

Coming into January of 2020, the momentum was starting to build again. We had gone live with Publishizer, and now I was operating a crowdfunding platform for authors, as well as a publishing company. After my former team members had left, I came to realize that I didn't actually need to hire their replacements. I needed to be fully aware of what was going on in my business and make the executive decisions to move all our active projects forward. In a sense it was keeping things simple, not delegating to middle managers or dissociating from any problems brewing. The authors I was working with had a special scheduling link and had permission to book a call whenever they desired. On each call we would accomplish whatever we needed and set up action steps for the next steps in their publishing process or for scheduling a promotion for their book. So, in another sense, I let my authors feel empowered to connect with their publisher whenever they wanted and let that drive a good part of my daily schedule.

Once the deal with Publishizer was done, Guy, the founding CEO, stepped down. In turn, my contacts at the platform were the co-founder, Lee, who lived in Bali, and a literary agent, Julia Guirado, who lives in Spain. The first call I had with Julia to talk about authors she was working with, I felt the sense of destiny at play. She is passionate, well-spoken, and absolutely loves working with authors through the publishing process. I felt right away that she was a great benefit to the deal, one I wasn't even tracking on when discussing all the deal points leading up to the takeover. Lee and I had a productive relationship, and he clearly cared about the platform and knew how to work it from every angle. Accordingly, he was my main point of contact, and we set a strategic plan for the year together. One of the main areas we focused on was running themed contests. We'd spend a month promoting a business contest, get the authors' crowdfunding campaigns ready, then, the next month, the authors would compete to see who could raise the most funds (i.e., pre-sell the most books) for their campaign. The winners would get prizes and special attention to connect them with a publisher. This turned out to be a pretty effective strategy, and over the course of the year, we ran five contests that brought in the majority of the $400,000-plus in sales that Publishizer generated.

While these contests were running every couple months, I was also at work developing another partnership with a company called The Author Incubator. They ran a whole program for first-time authors who were coached through the writing process and taken all the way through to having a publish-ready manuscript. We had done a trial with three books at the end of 2019, and both parties felt like it was a good working relationship, so we scaled it up in 2020. Where they worked in batches of four to seven authors per month, we soon started receiving dozens of books that were ready to publish from this partnership. We were receiving around $4,000 in revenue for each book, and then I would lead a group call with the authors and map out the whole publishing timeline for when their books would come out through Lifestyle Entrepreneurs Press. This partnership brought in over 25 books and over $125,000 of upfront revenue over the course of the year, and it was the first time I was working with authors who had a completed book. Up to this point, I was pretty involved with all the books we published. I would work with the author for months, if not over a year, leading up to calling a book "finished" and getting ready to go to print.

Of course, there was a lot going on in the broader world in 2020 too. When businesses closed and everyone was staying home, it was like a dam burst and every author who had been putting off writing their book suddenly made it a top priority. At least, that's what it felt like, as the year was simply explosive from the standpoint of signing new authors. It took me four years in book publishing to have 50 book deals signed. In 2020, we signed 55 new authors to the press! The Author Incubator was sending us books every month for the first half of the year, and Publishizer was doing close to $100,000 of revenue each month we had a contest running. It's worth pointing out that 70 percent of the funds raised were available to the author, so while we had lots of money coming in the door, a good chunk of it was earmarked to pay out to authors some number of months later. My goal was to sign deals with a number of the Publishizer authors for $10,000 each and be able to keep that revenue while adding another author to our roster and book to our catalog.

In 2019, I was getting my handle on the Ingram distribution relationship and really enjoyed flying out to Nashville every few months to present our forthcoming titles and build more relationships with the team. In 2020, those meetings all switched to virtual presentations. There wasn't the same level of connection since there were no off-the-cuff conversations or nights out with the team to get to know each other on a more personal level. I do feel fortunate that I got to put in a good amount of face time before switching over to virtual meetings, however, and on more than one occasion the Ingram team shared that they were impressed with how many book deals we were signing. In 2020 we started to sell a lot more books, both from the back catalog of books we had already published, and from new releases alike.

On top of all this, the core business of meeting with authors, aligning our vision for how to support them through the publishing process, then signing deals was still active in addition to these new acquisition channels. 2020 was accordingly my best year in business. On an accrual basis we broke the seven-figure mark at $1,041,472 in gross revenue. It was an amazing turnaround from losing my team, taking a hit to my confidence, and suffering the first year of declining revenues since starting the business. I was working diligently every day, usually on the phone for seven to nine hours in meetings Tuesday-Friday, with Monday as a flexible day for business planning, meeting with strategic partners, and still taking some author calls for anything important that came up on Mondays too. Overall, I can say that my level of focus increased dramatically and I matured into more of a business leader alongside my always-evolving skills of working with authors through the whole publishing process. All of this being the case, the business was still pretty expensive to run, and I was becoming highly skilled at playing high-interest lenders off one another and revolving through credit facilities with loan amounts between $70,000 to $125,000 each. 2020 was, therefore, a year when everything exploded at once; signing new authors, running a crowdfunding platform, hitting our stride with Ingram as a distributor, and cycling through debt and credit cards in a wave-like pattern.

Here is an excerpt from the end-of-year email I sent to our audience that was now over 25,000 in size:

Never have I been more clear, decisive, and aligned with the vision and mission I've set out for Lifestyle Entrepreneurs Press as 2020:

To Elevate Global Consciousness by Empowering Authors & Entrepreneurs. We are the Publisher for the Passionate and Help You Change the World with Your Words.

So many times I've leaned in this year to help and support; from countless strategic guidance sessions with our authors to help them navigate the year, to giving away free books to our audience to stay inspired, and consulting with entrepreneurial friends whose businesses were being rocked.

We also ran a number of contests on the Publishizer platform, which allowed our team to serve and support hundreds of authors...many more than I could work with directly in publishing partnership.

Our authors that stayed the course and leaned in to support their audiences saw considerable book sales and business growth, which, of course, is a reflection of the positive impact they are making in the world.

So, on this final day of 2020, I bid farewell to what was undoubtedly the most wild and crazy year I've experienced.

The world changed in 2020.

And that isn't just going to stop once the clock strikes midnight tonight.

We are all in for a wild ride next year, so my advice is plan accordingly.

Take this opportunity to get real with yourself about what you want to accomplish next year.

Get real with yourself about who you want to be and how you want to show up for those important to you next year.

Get real with yourself about what you're really here on Earth to do.

Is it to play it safe and be on the defensive, wary of dangers and threats coming in from seemingly all directions?

Or is it to play a bigger game, to make a real difference by inspiring others with your bold action?

Fortunes are made and the future is written by those who take decisive action in the face of uncertainty.

Spoiler alert: *There will always be uncertainty.*

So plan accordingly and chart your own course.

Stand firm in your choices

Let your inner voice guide you towards your own definition of Greatness

If you don't, someone else will guide you to theirs

You can take that to the bank.

Much love and see you next year,
Jesse

2021 All the Fun

2021 *All the Fun* is the name of a playlist I created over the course of the year. Every time I heard a song I liked, I would add it to the playlist and play those songs almost exclusively over the course of the year. It's a fitting name, as in many ways 2021 was a *lot* of fun. Coming into the year, I was riding on a high; the business I had started in my living room in Berkeley had made over a million dollars, and I was a couple years into our international distribution relationship with Ingram. I had bought a house in Las Vegas in 2018 and renovated over the course of 2019, which worked out well since I spent a lot of time in in throughout 2020 working practically non-stop.

By the end of 2020, a couple things had become clear. One was that while Publishizer brought in a lot of top-line revenue and allowed me exposure to a lot more authors, very few of them actually ended up signing a publishing deal with Lifestyle Entrepreneurs Press. Turns out one of the main reasons that authors ran crowdfunding campaigns was to attract interest from lots of publishers, and I found myself in a few awkward conversations when I'd talk to them about signing a deal and they learned I ran the platform as well as a publishing company. That was quite a different type of publishing consultation than I was used to, where authors already knew they wanted to work together and it was more about determining whether it was the right fit. The other thing that became clear was that while it was nice to receive four to seven ready-to-publish books each month from The Author Incubator, it wasn't nearly as enjoyable as working with an author through the whole publishing process and then celebrating together when their book was done and ready to publish. It was a good experiment, and I'm thankful for the partnership and opportunity, but we dialed it back towards the end of 2020 and eventually just focused on the books they had sent us and stopped taking on new ones.

So while Publishizer and The Author Incubator accounted for over a half a million dollars in revenue last year, going into 2021, we had unwound both partnerships and I re-focused on working directly with authors through the publishing process and signing them direct to our press, the way I had always done. Through my entire tenure running a book publishing company I have never worked through a literary agent or negotiated a publishing deal with a lawyer. There is something pure, clean, and enjoyable about having a one-on-one relationship with the author, establishing that we want to work together, and *then* bringing in support and resources to help make that happen.

Towards the end of 2020, the crypto markets were starting to heat up after a couple years of slumber. Some of my friends had tuned me into NFTs (non-fungible tokens), and I started following the space and placing some investments in the platforms that were launching these digital collectibles. Coming into 2021, these became the hottest commodities around. Crypto, overall, was on a massive bull run, and NFTs were a new-ish technology that was one part digital collectible and one part certificate of authenticity.

The nature of crypto Web3 technology is that every transaction can be seen on a public ledger (i.e., a blockchain). So you could see the chain of custody for every NFT, including what price it had sold at and what it was being offered for now. I started to get excited about the possibility of publishing books as NFTs and was looking into ways to make this happen.

A blockchain engineer that I had known for a number of years and had actually funded way back in 2013 when I was running University Incubator had approached me about being an advisor for his new startup. The idea evolved to become PowerFan, which had the mission to empower authors, artists, and creators to leverage blockchain technology in valuable new ways. After a few months of advising informally, he offered to quit his job and move to Vegas and have me on as a co-founder. Sensing that this was a "right place, right time" idea with crypto booming, I agreed. It started off pretty darn good; with crypto markets booming and NFTs a dominant narrative, almost everyone we talked to wanted to invest or partner with us. In just a few months, we raised over $500,000 at an insane valuation considering we didn't even have a product or token live yet. Nonetheless, mania ensued, and quickly I found myself working a lot on PowerFan and taking my eye of the ball of book publishing. Truthfully, I wanted to see them converge. Book publishing has always been a low-margin business. A book that costs $20 at retail can net $1 to $2, and it's capital-intensive to print and distribute physical books. I saw NFTs as a solution to that and a way to capture much higher margins. It all sounded good at the time.

As the year went on, the platform launched and we started launching a few NFT projects. Turns out it takes even more work to put together a NFT collection, get it ready to launch. and promote it then it does to publish a book. Not only that; it was (and is) still a new technology, and the general public doesn't intuitively understand how to buy a NFT the way someone knows to go on Amazon and order a book they like. So, there was a large educational component to drive each sale. But boom times make for fun times in business. Through to the end of the year crypto markets kept hitting new highs and it was a lot of fun for the first many months. Towards the end of the year, the founder went to Asia for some business development and to try and tap Asian demand for innovative crypto companies. Originally, he was heading there for a few weeks. But then he extended his stay. And extended it again. And then, as we moved into 2022, I came to grips with the fact that he may not come back. We were still having calls just about every day, but the fun of working together in person faded away to having Zoom calls after a day full of working with authors. By the time the crypto mania started to fade, I had a sobering realization that I had taken my eye off the ball with book publishing in a big way.

2022 And the Bills Come Due

Having unwound the Publishizer and Author Incubator partnerships going into 2021, a lot of revenue dried up accordingly. I thought we would sign a number of authors that ran crowdfunding campaigns, only to realize that even what I thought was a conservative estimate was overly optimistic. Cash started flowing out, and then it became a torrent as the hundreds of thousands raised from crowdfunding campaigns were paid out to authors. I had become so used to cycling through credit cards and high-interest business loans that it felt like second nature. That was all fine and good when tons of money was coming in the front door, but it was definitely not so good when money was mostly flowing the other way. To make matters worse, book retailers started returning books in increasingly larger volumes. In 2020 there was actually a boom in book orders. Makes sense, as people were at home and many devoured books in greater quantities than they did before. That translated to bigger book orders from retailers, which translated into bigger print runs for us as a publisher. In 2020 into 2021, book sales looked like they were exploding, and on paper they were. But towards the end of 2021, returns shot up over 300 percent, and we were getting back thousands upon thousands of books that I had already considered finished sales. Uh oh.

The nature of book publishing via in-store distribution is basically a glorified consignment model. Retailers like Amazon get a 50 to 60 percent wholesale discount from retail price, and they are allowed to return any or all of the books that don't sell through to the final customer for a full refund within six months. This time-delay effect masked what looked like a boom in sales. Then, right before the six-month mark, the returns would come in. The way our distribution deal worked with Ingram was everything was on a master account. Printing, shipping, in-store marketing expenses, and returns were all tallied up and accounted for before the bottom-line number of what we made as the publishing company. By the end of 2021, the tide had turned dramatically and returns were devouring our profit margin to the point of non-existence. Having been in the business at that point for seven years, I was all-in on trying to make this work. So what did I do? Took out more lines of credit and accessed as much working capital as possible to ride it out.

But the problem with having a low-margin business that is capital intensive is it takes a lot of revenue to generate a healthy net profit. By the end of the first quarter of 2022, the writing was on the wall. Continual returns of books we already printed and shipped wiped out any chance of getting paid for the books that did sell decent and weren't returned. A book that gets returned has been printed, shipped to a retailer, then shipped back to our warehouse; it incurs a re-stocking fee and deducts from net sales. In other words, it is more costly to have returns than to have never printed and shipped the book in the first place. This was compounded by the fact that I had spent considerable time and energy on a crypto startup and now the crypto market was tanking. Double uh oh.

In fairly short order it became crystal clear I needed to make some big decisions. So I talked to Ingram and asked if we could renegotiate our distribution relationship. I had built good relationships there and always loved working with their team, but now it was bleeding a hole in our balance sheet, and thankfully they allowed us to phase out of the terms of our deal sooner than contractually stipulated. As we began to plan for a transition out of the distribution relationship, I decided to tell our authors what was happening behind the scenes. Cash flow was becoming really tight and for the first time in a long time, I was worried we would actually run out. It was a painful thing to write over 100 authors and tell them that the business was failing. I gave them the option to ride it out with us, or that we would agree to release them from their publishing agreement and turn all the rights to their books back over to them.

When I had the email drafted and ready to send to our entire author base, the authors with whom I had gotten in the trenches and helped create and publish books for years and years, it hit me. I prayed and hung my head in a state of defeat, then hit send. Then I prayed some more. The responses started flying in within minutes. A mix of compassion, confusion, and requests to terminate publishing agreements. In a matter of weeks I shifted from believing I could find one more way to pull a proverbial rabbit from the hat to managing the unwinding of the business I built for close to a decade. It was a major mix of emotions, and it affected every author differently depending where they were in the process or how long their book had been published. With that first email I still had hope that there was a way through this. Just a few weeks later, it was clear that was not the case.

Despite accommodations from our distributor, an array of credit cards and financing, and a number of authors willing to ride it out and stick with me, it was soon over. Each week I watched our cash flowing out with barely any coming in. The writing was more than on the wall; the end was in sight like a freight train bearing down on me in a tunnel with nowhere to turn and no way out. Weeks after I sent the first email, I drafted a second a second email. This was by far the most difficult decision I've had to make in 20 years of entrepreneurship and 8 years of running a publishing company. Here is the letter I sent to our authors in June of 2022:

I hope this email finds you well, and I apologize in advance for being the bearer of bad news

This email is a formal acknowledgment of our situation at Lifestyle Entrepreneurs Press and how it affects you as an author.

It is with great sadness that I write to inform you that the company will be winding down and proceeding through a bankruptcy and insolvency process effective immediately.

Over the last two years, and especially over the last few months, the business has experienced difficulties that prevent us from continuing, despite numerous attempts to avert this situation and at great expense.

It has been over two years since we received any distribution of funds for books sold through retailers despite our best efforts. In the absence of receiving funds for book sales, we took on additional financing and debt to continue operations and pay royalties.

However, as that debt load is now in the multiple six figures, and it is now clear that we will not be receiving any funds from our former distributor, the only realistic option is to face the situation and wind down operations.

As you're likely aware, inflation is at its highest level in 40 years and there have been significant supply chain issues since early 2020. In addition to managing through rising costs, delays, and materials shortages, we experienced our returns increase by 300% in this time.

Through each sequential issue, we managed to find a way forward, often at considerable cost. Holding out hope for a change in fortunes has proven unbearably expensive, as well as mentally and emotionally exhausting.

After eight years in business, we have reached the end of the road, and it is deeply saddening to acknowledge that giving my personal best, and our best as a company, hasn't been enough.

Therefore, this event of corporate insolvency activates the Termination clause of our Publishing Agreement.

Accordingly, all rights to your book are hereby returned to you as we wind down the business through the bankruptcy process and proceedings.

Should you wish to continue making your book available through self-publishing, we will provide files for your book without our publishing information or logo on them.

If you would like these files, please write Tracey on my team and they will be prepared and delivered.

However, even if you do nothing, your book will remain available for sale for a limited time based on the amount of inventory currently with retailers. This reflects the termination terms of our agreement with our former distribution partner.

I realize this may come as a surprise or a shock, and I would like to take this opportunity to say I am deeply sorry that the situation has come to this.

On behalf of our publishing team, it has been an honor to work with you in the time we had. With sincere apologies,

Jesse

The Aftermath and a New Beginning

I take 100 percent responsibility for what transpired. It's not pretty and it certainly wasn't fun. It took many months to navigate through the unwinding of the business I spent eight years building and to the greatest degree possible I tried to make everyone whole. Some authors lost out on a couple quarters of book royalties. Some authors whose books hadn't come out yet suddenly found themselves in limbo. I had put everything I had into the business and had personally guaranteed a considerable amount of the financing we took on. It's going to take me some time to recover and rebuild after this level of wholesale financial devastation. Yet I have still found some solace through such destruction;, a number of authors wrote me heart-warming letters or called and told me how much they appreciated the support my team and I gave them. My team witnessed the whole process unfold and stood by me, helping transition books and files back to authors, even when I couldn't pay them for a time. For close to eight years of running Lifestyle Entrepreneurs Press, one thing I was most proud of was never missing payroll. That came to an end as the business wound down, and it was a tough pill to swallow, a sort of final acknowledgement that it really was over.

For around a month I was in a void, floating in limbo. I set my ego completely aside and had one humbling conversation after another with authors, partners, team members, family, and friends. It was like emerging from a tornado of activity, getting whipped around in all directions to waking up in the aftermath and seeing the devastated foundations of what used to feel like home. I turned my consciousness inward and started meditating. I simplified my life and cut out all extraneous expenses. I went home to visit my family and walked along the streets where I grew up, marveling at the passage of time and the lifetimes of experience that had transpired since I was a boy. I faced myself in the mirror and reaffirmed that I love and accept myself just the way I am. I chose to find meaning in what seemed like madness and to not self-destruct. I have seen first-hand how losing a business can precede losing one's mind. For a time it felt like an open wound. And then, as weeks and months passed, even though the scars are still visible, the bleeding stopped.

A raging forest fire can burn wild and out of control. But when the flames eventually subside and the smoldering ashes are subject to inevitable rain, they become the fertilizer for future growth. Out of the wreckage, I have realized that I still very much love working with authors. I still very much love books and believe they are the building blocks for knowledge and wisdom to be transmitted through society and generations. I still very much have the skill set that was sharpened across a decade of both being an author and working closely with over 100 published authors. And so, now that the flames have subsided and the rains have fallen, there are new green shoots appearing across the horizon.

A handful of my former team felt the same way—that they love working with authors and wanted to see how we could continue to do so. From some heart-to-heart conversations we decided to launch a consultancy and become partners. The Publishing Consultants LLC was born, and now we work together in a new way. Instead of trying to manage the publishing relationship for life, we offer publishing support as a service. We can work with authors that have a manuscript and guide it through to completion with editorial support, design, layout, formatting, website development, and marketing. But now the end result is either setting their book up for self-publishing or introducing them to a publisher to handle the printing, distribution, logistics, and royalties.

In a real coming-full-circle moment, I had a call with David Hancock, the CEO of Morgan James Publishing, who has been *my* publisher for *Lifestyle Entrepreneur* since 2014 and who helped me get our first distribution deal many years ago. I told him what happened, and he offered his deep and sincere condolences. When the conversation turned to what I might do next, it turns out we were both thinking along the same lines. He offered me a position, and I am now pleased to say that I am the Associate Publisher at Morgan James Publishing, where I have been able to help migrate a number of books and authors I previously worked with into their catalog. This allowed a number of our authors to continue on with full in-store distribution and gives me the opportunity to bring new authors to the table for publishing consideration. From pitching David on my book at the VIP reception of an author event in Las Vegas so many years ago, we have grown to be friends and it's a pleasure to have landed at Morgan James. Truthfully, I don't think I would have taken a publishing position anywhere else. And truthfully, I didn't even look. I'm happy to be a part of the team that brought my first book into reality.

As I write these words now, it dawns on me that we have arrived at the present moment. This moment is indeed a present, and each day in life is a gift to be unwrapped and enjoyed. Being an entrepreneur my entire adult life, that is very much how it feels. When I started writing my first book, I had just extricated myself from a very uncomfortable situation; feeling cornered between running a company I was trying to sell while a full-time student at UC Berkeley. When that situation resolved and I was on a plane to China for the summer, I knew it was time to write. In the ten years since I saw that through to writing a bestselling book, becoming a publisher, and publishing over 125 books on entrepreneurship, health and wellness, self-help, and spirituality. Now that epic experience is in the rearview mirror, and in the aftermath I knew it was time to write once again. For so many years I wondered if I'd ever write a second book. Now I know the answer. I hope you have enjoyed it and I extend my sincere gratitude that you made it to the end!

What happens now is a modern-day choose your own adventure. You can close this book and carry on with your life, hopefully entertained and inspired. Or you can choose to start that business you've been thinking of, or write that book that you've always wanted to write. If that is your choice, it would be an honor to meet you, and I welcome the opportunity to support you on your journey as an author and entrepreneur.

No matter what you choose, I hope you choose to embrace each day with passion and life live to the fullest, because at the end of the day, making that choice each day is what makes life worth living. May it always be so.

With love,
Jesse

Epilogue

I'm sitting on my crushed blue velvet couch in my home in Las Vegas, cuddled up with my sweetheart Valeria. We met the day after I started writing this book and on our second date I asked if she would be my creative muse. I had never asked someone to be my muse before, and fortunately for me she said yes. I took her hand, kissed it gently and thanked her sincerely. 10 weeks later I put the finishing touches on this 65,000+ word book! Throughout the process we would do "Books & Bubbles" nights, where we'd get a bottle of Prosecco, put it on ice, and sip it while I read her the latest chapter drafts. I'm smiling now as I know soon enough I'll be reading this to her and it will warm her heart.

This has been the wildest year of my life, and by now you're well aware that I've had a few wild years over the last couple decades. But just like a wildfire can decimate the forest it rages through, in its wake is rich fertilizer for the next season of new growth. Out of the ashes, green sprouts appear. The endless dance of life is both creation and destruction, this is the cycle that entrepreneurship follows as well. To be an entrepreneur is to ride the waves of creation and destruction. The creative part is the fun part, the glorified aspect of being an entrepreneur. The destructive part is the undercurrent that sucks the water back out to the ocean, just to be gathered again by a new wave rolling in. What I have come to appreciate over 20 years of travel, adventure and starting businesses is that as long as we're still alive, there is another wave to ride.

While the end of this book marks the end of a decade in book publishing, it also marks a new beginning. When I think of how my life will look 10 years from now, it's a wide open field of possibility. Just as there's no way I could have foreseen my current life situation when I put the finishing touches on my first book ten years ago, I know there will be plenty of surprises, adventures and unexpected plot twists still to come. To me that is exciting. To me that gives hope and purpose. Who knows, maybe I won't wait another ten years to write my next book!

Thank you for taking this journey with me and I truly hope you enjoyed it.

Feel free to reach out and drop me a line: Jesse@JesseKrieger.com

Wishing you happiness and success in all you do.

Special Thanks

I would like to extend my special thanks to you for reading this book! Thanks to my parents, my sister and family for wonderful support over the years and a spirit of adventurousness. Thanks to those who have inspired me and those with whom I've shared formative experiences. Thanks to my publishing team for helping make countless books a reality, Tracey Ashby, Julia Guirado, Eldin Rodic, Leo Schiavina, Zora Knauf, Irena Kalcheva, Stan Kurkula and all the partners supported over the years.

Thanks to my publishing mentors and partners, Adrian Kok and Carol Lin at Kanyin Publications, David Hancock at Morgan James Publishing, the Ingram Publisher Services team that helped us get books into stores and often amused at my antics.

Thanks to Valeria Ofarril for being my creative muse and partner

Thank you, thank you, thank you

www.ingramcontent.com/pod-product-compliance
Lightning Source LLC
Chambersburg PA
CBHW070119100426
42744CB00010B/1871

9781953153982